Revision for Criminal Law
(Offences against the person)
Sally Russell LLB (Hons), PGCE

Revision summaries, exercises and examination practice for criminal law, offences against the person, complete with answers and example examination scripts.

Free interactive exercises at www.drsr.org

Based on the law and cases in my 2013 Kindle book A2 Law for AQA Unit 3A, this text will, however, be useful for other criminal law courses, including OCR, Ilex and LLB. It covers revision of the following areas:

Murder (including *actus reus* and *mens rea* generally)

Voluntary manslaughter (loss of control and diminished responsibility)

Involuntary manslaughter (gross negligence and unlawful act manslaughter)

Non-fatal offences against the person (assault, battery, actual and grievous bodily harm, wounding with intent)

Defences (insanity, automatism, intoxication, consent and self-defence)

Examination questions and answer guides are based on AQA examination papers. A comparable OCR question has been included for the evaluation examination practice in each subject chapter. For further guidance on what else might be needed for these go to the OCR website at www.ocr.org and look at the mark schemes, ('I want to' then 'Download past papers'). These are extremely comprehensive and contain all you need to know.

Other books by Sally Russell

As new books may be available by the time you read this I have not listed my other books by title. They currently include crime and tort at AS level, crime, tort and concepts of law for both the AQA and OCR examination board at A2 level and various books in *'the law explained'* series. For the most up to date list of what is available please check my author's page on Amazon or visit my website at www.drsr.org. All my books are available in both Kindle and paperback format.

About the author

Sally Russell was formerly head of law at a sixth-form college, a senior examiner for AQA and tort advisor for the Institute of Legal Executive Tutorial College. She has written various materials for both teachers and students, for Pearson Education, Hodder education and the National Extension College. She is also a regular contributor to the A-Level Law Review. For more information visit www.drsr.org

Introduction

My main objective has been to combine legal accuracy with a style that is accessible to all students, so I hope you will find this book both stimulating and helpful. Fully updated with recent cases and laws it is written in a lively, clear and accessible way and is designed to help students of all learning styles to understand the subject.

Although aimed at A-Level the books provide a good base for 1st Year LLB, ILEX and other courses, and can be used as self-study guides.

Each Chapter contains **examples** to help you see how the law relates to real life situations; ***tasks*** and ***self-test questions***, to help you check your understanding, as well as **examination tips** and **application practice** to help you prepare for problem questions. Where applicable the books also contain **tips and guidance on evaluating** the law to help with essay questions. **Summaries** and **diagrams** help to make the law clear.

The '*the law explained*' series offers a more in-depth coverage of individual areas with additional tasks, examples and examination practice. This means you can pick those topics for which you need more guidance (all the answers are included in the book).

For a range of free interactive exercises please go to www.drsr.org and click on 'Free Exercises' to see what's available.

Table of Contents

Revision 1 Murder

Murder is the unlawful killing of a human being. It can be committed not only by a positive act but also by omission. In **Gibbins and Proctor 1918**, the D's lived together with the man's daughter. They failed to give her food and she died. The court held that where food was withheld with intent to cause grievous bodily harm then it would be murder if this caused death. The CA upheld their murder convictions.

However, the courts do draw a distinction between an act and an omission. In **Airedale NHS Trust v Bland 1993**, discontinuing medical treatment was treated as an omission rather than a positive action. This was a civil case so is not strictly binding on the criminal courts. It will be highly persuasive though. The HL made clear that the **Bland** ruling would not apply to euthanasia, where there is a positive action by a doctor to bring about a patient's death.

In **Cox 1992**, a doctor gave a lethal injection to a patient begging for help to die. This is a positive act, and so amounts to murder.

Here is a recap of *actus reus*

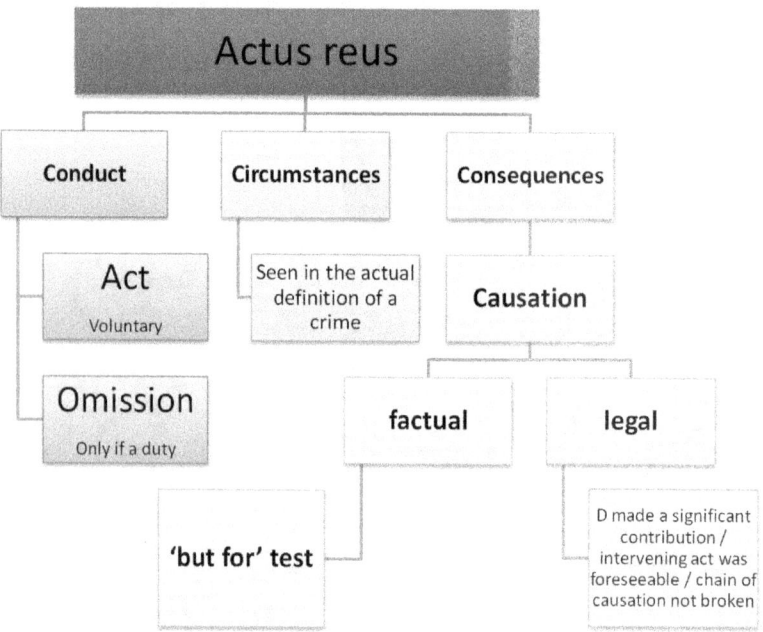

If the *actus reus* includes a consequence then the question of causation arises. This can be important in murder cases, as murder is a result crime. D's act or omission must cause the result (death) in fact and in law. The main points on causation are in the table below.

Factual causation

R v White 1910	'but for' his actions would she be alive? No, she would have died anyway so he did not cause that death.

Legal causation

R v Smith 1959	If D's act was an **operating and substantial** cause of death, there is no break in the chain of causation.
R v Cheshire 1991	Following **Smith**, if D has made a **significant contribution** to the death then hospital treatment will only break the chain of causation if it is **independent of the original act** and a potent cause in itself.
Roberts 1971 The prosecution relied on this case in **Corbett 1996**, to find that D caused the death of a victim who was hit and killed by a car when trying to escape from D's attack.	If the *victim's* act is **foreseeable**, it will not break the chain of causation, as long as it is not 'daft'.
R v Pagett 1983	If a *third party's* act is **foreseeable** it will not break the chain of causation and the police returning fire was a **natural consequence** of D's actions.

Exercise 1 Case studies on Mellor 1996 / Corbett 1996

In **Mellor 1996**, an elderly man was taken to hospital following an attack in which he suffered broken ribs and other injuries. He died from bronchial-pneumonia brought on by his injuries. The hospital had failed to give him oxygen which may have saved him. The CA held that if D's act made a significant contribution, it was immaterial whether incompetence or mistaken treatment was also a significant contributory factor. In **Corbett 1996**, the victim was trying to escape an attack by D, when he fell and was hit by a car. The court held that the question was whether the victim's actions were within a 'range of foreseeability'. If so the chain of causation was not broken, as was the case here.

What could arguably have broken the chain of causation in **Mellor**?

In which 1991 case did the court rule that as long as D's act was a significant and operative cause it need not be the sole cause?

How do the rules on factual and legal causation apply to **Mellor**?

Which case would you use in support of the decision in **Corbett** and why?

Sometimes questions arise about whether someone who is 'brain dead' or a foetus in the womb is a human being. In **AGs Reference (No 3 of 1994) 1997**, the HL held that a foetus was not a human being for the purpose of a murder conviction. However, if the foetus is injured and dies from that injury after being born, that could amount to murder.

In Coke's 18th Century definition of murder, the unlawful killing must be done with 'malice aforethought'. This expression is still used but has been interpreted as meaning with intention.

In **Vickers 1957**, the CA held that the *mens rea* for murder is satisfied by either an intention to kill, or an intention to cause grievous bodily harm. This was confirmed by the HL in **DPP v Smith 1960**.

Intent may be direct (D's aim or purpose) or indirect. The latter, also called oblique intent, is where there is a virtual certainty that death or serious injury will result and D appreciates that this is the case. This test was stated in **Nedrick** by the CA and confirmed by the HL in **Woollin 1998**.

Exercise 2 Case Study on mens rea

In **Stringer 2008**, a boy had been accused of murder and arson after a fire started in his house at the bottom of the stairs. Several of his family were sleeping upstairs at the time and his brother died in the fire. There was evidence that he had started the fire, although he denied this.

The boy was only 14 with a low IQ. He argued that he did not have the required intent for murder.

The CA confirmed **Woollin** and held that the distinction between the two parts of the test should be made clear to the jury. However, if this test was applied to the facts of the case there was clear evidence for the jury to find intent. There could only be one answer to the first part and even with his age and low IQ the second part of the test would also be satisfied.

What is the first part of the **Woollin** test?

How would it be applied to the facts in **Stringer**?

What is the second part of the **Woollin** test?

How would this be applied to the facts in **Stringer**?

It would seem that the test is one of evidence not proof. In which case was this restated after **Woollin**?

Examination tip

Remember to be selective. A question on murder may well include *actus reus, mens rea* or the partial defences leading to a manslaughter, rather than murder, conviction – but very rarely all of these. If something is obvious discuss it very briefly, e.g., you could say that there is clear intent to kill so no question of *mens rea* and so move quickly on to the other issues. Alternatively, you could say that the issue of causation is clear but it may be difficult to prove intent and so discuss *mens rea* and the **Nedrick** test in more detail.

Exercise 3 Note the principle of the following cases

Fagan

Stone and Dobinson

Roberts

Cheshire

DPP v Smith

Blaue

In **Inglis 2010**, a mother was convicted of murder and sentenced to life imprisonment for killing her severely disabled son. There was clear intent to kill, so even though she acted in what she believed were her son's best interests the charge was murder. This can be compared with **Gilderdale** heard in the same week. Here a woman killed her daughter who had a chronic illness and who had tried to commit suicide herself on several occasions. She was cleared of attempted murder by a jury (attempted murder because it could not be shown if the drugs she gave caused the death or not). Again, she intended to kill her daughter so the charge had to be murder, but the jury were clearly sympathetic.

In 2006 The Law Commission recommended a three-tier structure of first and second degree murder and manslaughter. Only the first would mean a mandatory life sentence. These recommendations have not been taken up.

Summary of the actus reus and mens rea of murder

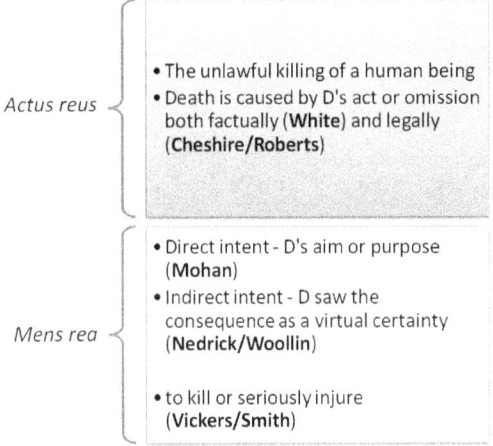

Actus reus
- The unlawful killing of a human being
- Death is caused by D's act or omission both factually (**White**) and legally (**Cheshire/Roberts**)

Mens rea
- Direct intent - D's aim or purpose (**Mohan**)
- Indirect intent - D saw the consequence as a virtual certainty (**Nedrick/Woollin**)

- to kill or seriously injure (**Vickers/Smith**)

The law on *actus reus* and *mens rea* prepares you for answering a murder 'problem' question. Murder can be committed by an omission (**Gibbins & Proctor**); it is a result crime so it must be proved that D's act caused death factually (**White**) and in law (**Cheshire/Roberts**); the *mens rea* of murder is intent which can be direct (**Mohan**) or indirect (**Nedrick/Woollin**).

Examination tip

In all problem questions you need to take a logical approach. First read the facts carefully and then state and apply the law in a logical manner, using cases in support in order to reach a sustainable conclusion. As practice for an exam question, try this with the case of **Pagett**.

Exercise 4 Application practice

Read the facts of **Pagett** and then use your knowledge of the *actus reus* and *mens rea* of murder to apply the law to these facts.

Exercise 5 Evaluation practice

This exercise will provide you with a sound base for an essay/evaluation question.

Look at the brief comments below and expand on each to produce a paragraph. State the current law with a case example, followed by a short critique of the law, including any reforms or proposed reforms if appropriate.

The law on intent lacks clarity

The serious harm rule should be changed

Mercy killing should be made legal

The mandatory sentence for murder should be abolished

Self-test questions

What is the actus reus *and* mens rea *of murder, and how have the courts interpreted the latter?*

What is a result crime and what is the significance in terms of actus reus*?*

Can you explain the law on causation using two murder cases?

In which CA case was the 'virtual certainty' test for mens rea *established, and which HL case confirmed this?*

Exercise 6 Examination practice

Despite some recent reforms, there are still criticisms to be made of the current law on murder and voluntary manslaughter. Consider relevant criticisms of that law, and suggest any reforms that may be appropriate. (25 Marks)

N.B: This question is repeated in the next chapter as it covers both murder and voluntary manslaughter. Separate guides are given in the answers at the end of this book for each area (see Answers 1 and Answers2).

A similar OCR question for June 2012 in relation to murder

The *mens rea* for murder is too complicated both in theory and practice. It needs to be simplified by Parliament.

Discuss the extent to which this statement is accurate (50 marks)

For a range of free interactive exercises please go to www.drsr.org and click on 'Free Exercises' to see what's available.

The first thing to remember is that the two special defences of loss of control and diminished responsibility only apply to murder. They are called partial defences because they do not lead to an acquittal but to a conviction for manslaughter rather than murder, thus allowing the judge to use discretion when sentencing. Note also that 'voluntary' and 'involuntary' are legal terms, used to distinguish between manslaughter following a murder charge, and manslaughter as a separate charge. There is no such charge as 'voluntary manslaughter' or 'involuntary manslaughter'. The first would be charged as murder, the second as manslaughter.

Loss of control

This defence comes under **s 54** and **s 55** of the **Coroners and Justice Act 2009**. **S 54** states:

> *'(1) Where a person ("D") kills or is a party to the killing of another ("V"), D is not to be convicted of murder if —*
>
> *(a) D's acts and omissions in doing or being a party to the killing resulted from D's loss of self-control,*
>
> *(b) the loss of self-control had a qualifying trigger, and*
>
> *(c) a person of D's sex and age, with a normal degree of tolerance and self-restraint and in the circumstances of D, might have reacted in the same or in a similar way to D.'*

The 'qualifying trigger' under **s 54(1)(b)** refers to whether something triggered D's loss of control – and what that something was. **S 55(1)** of the Act sets out the qualifying triggers. The loss of control must be triggered by:

> *D's fear of serious violence from V against D or another identified person; or*
>
> *a thing or things done or said (or both) which –*
>
> *(a) constituted circumstances of an extremely grave character, and*
>
> *(b) caused D to have a justifiable sense of being seriously wronged.*
>
> *Or a combination of both of these*

So there are three things to consider:

did D lose self-control?

was the loss of self-control triggered by something specified in s 55?

would a normal person of D's sex and age have reacted in the same way in D's circumstances?

Did D lose control?

There must be loss of control not just self-restraint. In **Cocker 1989**, D had finally given way to his wife's entreaties to ease her pain and end her life. His defence failed as the evidence showed he had not lost control. This would still apply for the new law.

The triggers

Fear of serious violence would apply in the case of women who fear violent abuse, as in **Thornton & Aluwahlia.**

The violence need not be directed at D. In **Pearson 1992**, a boy killed his father because of the father's ill treatment, not of himself but of his brother, and the defence succeeded. **S 55** refers to fear of violence against D or 'another identified person' so this is still the case.

Loss of control can be caused by both actions and words, 'things done and said'. However, **s 55** adds that these must be 'extremely grave' and 'justifiably' cause D to feel 'seriously' wronged.

In **Parker 2012**, the day after an argument when he had punched her, D's wife sent him a text saying she wanted to separate and he should pack up his things and leave the family home. When she later went home, he stabbed her repeatedly, within a short time of her arriving. He argued that the text message had come 'as a bolt from the blue' and he had 'lost it' when she told him she didn't love him. The judge left the defence of loss of control to the jury but it was rejected. In dismissing D's appeal the CA held that the matters he had relied on could not reasonably be treated by any jury as circumstances of an extremely grave character which caused him to have a justifiable sense that he had been seriously wronged.

Would a normal person react in a similar way?

In **Holley 2005**, the Privy Council held that D was to be judged against the standard of a person having 'ordinary powers of self-control', not against the standard expected of a particular D in the same position. The Act follows this line of thought. **S 54(1)(c)** refers to 'a person of D's sex and age, with a normal degree of tolerance and self-restraint and in the circumstances of D'. This is further clarified by **s 54(3)** which allows for 'reference to all of D's circumstances other than those whose only relevance to D's conduct is that they bear on D's general capacity for tolerance or self-restraint'.

Examples of what can't be attributed to a person of D's age and sex include exceptional excitability, and obsession (stated *obiter* in **Smith 2000**), as well as drugs and alcohol (**Holley**). These would be matters that only related to D's capacity for tolerance and self-restraint.

In **Asmelash 2013**, D had been drinking with another man and got into a fight, during which D stabbed and killed him. He said the deceased had made him so angry that he lost control. The judge applied **s 54** and said the jury should consider whether a person of D's sex and age with a normal degree of tolerance and self-restraint and in the same circumstances, but unaffected by alcohol, would have reacted in the same or similar way. D was convicted and appealed. The CA agreed with the judge that the consumption of alcohol should be ignored.

Differences with the new law against the old law of provocation include:

S 54(2) states that the loss of self-control does not need to be sudden

S 54(4) states that the defence is not allowed if D acted in a 'considered desire for revenge'

S 54(1)(b) states that there must be a qualifying trigger. Under the old law, there was no specific restriction on what caused D to lose control

S 55(6) excludes sexual infidelity as a qualifying trigger

The Law Commission had advised not keeping the loss of control requirement and this is understandable considering the desire to extend the defence to 'battered women' cases such as **Thornton**.

Revenge is usually carried out after a period of time, so the defence could have failed under the old law because the loss of control had to be 'sudden and temporary', now it could fail because revenge is excluded by the Act.

Sexual infidelity is excluded as a trigger but the original law of provocation was passed to give a defence to exactly that type of situation. The LC did not recommend including this restriction and it has been limited somewhat by the decision in **Clinton 2012** that sexual infidelity could be taken into account as part of the overall circumstances.

- ## D's conduct resulted from a loss of self-control – S 54(1)(a)

- ## The loss of control had a qualifying trigger – S 54(1)(b)

- ## A person of D's age and sex with an ordinary level of tolerance and self-restraint may have done similarly in the circumstances – S 54(1)(c)

Exercise 7

In September 2010, shortly before the new law came into force, the Daily Mail, referring to the **Thornton** case, wrote that under the new rules, "it is highly unlikely she would have been convicted of murder" because of the removal of the sudden and temporary rule.

Is this true?

In the same article it was stated that the new law "means husbands will no longer be able to claim that infidelity was the spur for their actions".

In which case did judges interpret the Act so that this may not be fully excluded but can be taken into account as part of the circumstances in which D acted?

The above sentence continued with "and will face a charge of murder, rather than manslaughter".

Can you see anything wrong with this statement?

Briefly explain whether the loss of control defence is likely to succeed or fail if the following cases were tried under the new law.

Baillie 1995

Doughty 1986

Exercise 8 Case study

In **Clinton 2011**, D killed his wife, who had told him she was having an affair, and was convicted of murder. The evidence was that he had planned the death having done some research on the internet. He later killed his wife during a heated exchange and claimed both loss of control and diminished responsibility. The jury rejected the latter defence so the case continued on the basis of loss of control. The judge then held that the evidence showed that there was no loss of control due to one of the 'qualifying triggers' as required by the **Coroners' and Justice Act**, and said that the wife's infidelity should be ignored as this was specifically excluded by the Act. However, in **Clinton 2012**, the CA held that the judge had misdirected herself about the possible relevance of the wife's infidelity. The totality of the matters relied on as a qualifying trigger should be considered and all the circumstances taken together. In this case, the sexual infidelity was an integral part of the whole and the circumstances as a whole had had sufficient impact on D to suggest the defence should have been put to the jury. A retrial was ordered.

Which section of the **Coroners' and Justice Act** excludes sexual infidelity as a trigger?

What are acceptable triggers for the loss of control?

Why did the judge say the wife's infidelity should be ignored?

Did the CA agree?

What effect might sexual infidelity have even though excluded by the Act?

Why did the CA order a retrial?

Diminished responsibility

This defence still comes under **s 2** of the **Homicide Act** but is amended by **s 52** of the **Coroners and Justice Act**. Much of the terminology is the same or similar, so older cases will still be used when interpreting the law.

There must be an 'abnormality of mental functioning' which must arise from a recognised medical condition, substantially impair D's responsibility to do one of three things and provide an explanation for D's acts and omissions in doing or being a party to the killing.

Abnormality of mental functioning

This means something that reasonable people would term abnormal – **Byrne 1960**.

An abnormality caused by alcoholism (a medical condition) may be accepted as diminished responsibility – **Tandy 1989**. Intoxication in itself will not (**Dowds 2012**).

Where there is evidence of intoxication as well as another cause of 'abnormality' the jury should ignore the intoxication – **Dietschmann 2003**.

Recognised medical condition

D will need medical evidence to support the defence. The burden of proof (unlike with loss of control) is on D, who must prove diminished responsibility. The standard of proof is the balance of probabilities.

Substantially impair D's responsibility to do one of three things

The 'abnormality of mental functioning' must substantially impair D's ability to:

> **understand the nature of his conduct; or**
>
> **form a rational judgement; or**
>
> **exercise self-control.**

This impairment need not be total but must be more than trivial – **Lloyd 1967**.

Provides an explanation for D's acts and omissions

This means that there must now be some causal connection between D's abnormality of mental functioning and the conduct. The abnormality must cause the killing or make a significant contribution to it.

For a range of free interactive exercises please go to www.drsr.org and click on 'Free Exercises' to see what's available.

Summary of the defence of diminished responsibility

Abnormality of mental functioning: will be interpreted as for abnormality of mind ...	... so different from that of ordinary human beings that the reasonable man would term it abnormal **Byrne 1960**
Substantially impaired	Impairment need not be total but must be more than trivial or minimal **Lloyd 1967**
It is D's ability to do one of three things which must be substantially impaired	These are: to understand the nature of his conduct; to form a rational judgement; to exercise self-control.
Alcoholism, or alcohol dependency syndrome, may lead to a successful defence but only if the first drink was involuntary	**Tandy 1989/Wood 2008**
If D is intoxicated *as well as* suffering from a abnormality of mental functioning the defence may succeed, but the jury must ignore the intoxication	**Dietschmann 2003**
The **Coroners and Justice Act 2009** does not change the rules on intoxication	**Dowds 2012**
The abnormality of mental functioning must provide an explanation for D's conduct	A causation issue; did the abnormality of mental functioning cause D to act that way?

Exercise 9 Principles of law

State the case or section of an Act for the following principles of law:

The defence of loss of control is not allowed if D acted in a 'considered desire for revenge'.

The loss of self-control does not need to be sudden.

Sexual infidelity may be relevant to the circumstances of D, even though excluded by **s 55**.

An 'abnormality of mind' (now mental functioning) for diminished responsibility is one that reasonable people would term abnormal.

The abnormality of mental functioning must provide an explanation for D's acts and omissions in doing or being a party to the killing.

An abnormality caused by alcoholism may be accepted as diminished responsibility.

Impairment of responsibility need not be total but must be more than trivial.

Where there is evidence of intoxication as well as another cause of 'abnormality' the jury should ignore the intoxication.

Exercise 10 case study on Freaney

In **Freaney 2011**, a woman was cleared of the murder of her severely autistic 11-year-old son. Mrs Freaney denied murder but admitted manslaughter on the grounds of diminished responsibility. Her son needed 24-hour care and help with dressing, washing, brushing his teeth and eating. He was not toilet trained and still wore nappies. She murdered her son using her coat belt and when she was sure he was dead she lay down on the bed beside him and tried to commit suicide. The jury decided she was suffering under extreme mental stress at the time she strangled her son Glen with a coat belt. Her plea of diminished responsibility was accepted and in July 2011 she was sentenced to a supervision order.

What was Mrs Freaney charged with and what did she plead in defence?

What is the effect of a successful defence and why is that important for D?

What must be proved for the amended defence?

How would you apply the new law to this case?

Examination tip

As these offences only apply once there is a murder charge, you should first note that D may have committed this offence. If the issues of intent and causation are clear you only need a very brief discussion of murder, but then go on to suggest that D may be able to rely on one or both of these defences. You will often have to discuss both defences, as there is an overlap between them.

So how do these two defences now apply in practice? Let's look at an earlier case and apply the law as it is now.

Application of the law

Applying the new law to Thornton we could say that she could argue the defence of diminished responsibility under the **Homicide Act 1957 s 2(1)** as amended by the **Coroners and Justice Act 2009**. She had an abnormality of mental functioning arising from 'battered woman' syndrome which is a recognised medical condition. This must have substantially impaired (substantial being not trivial but not necessarily total, **Lloyd**) her ability to understand the nature of her conduct, to form a rational judgement, or to exercise self-control. In this case, she would most likely rely on the last of these, as it seems she understood the nature of her conduct and was sufficiently rational to go into the kitchen and get a knife. If it is believed that she was unable to exercise self-control due to her abnormality then the defence of diminished responsibility may succeed. It is also possible that she could argue loss of control under **s 54** and **55** of the **Coroners and Justice Act 2009**. This requires a loss of self-control, which had a qualifying trigger and would have caused a person of her sex and age to react in a similar way in the circumstances. She could fall at the first hurdle, as it is necessary to show that she lost control. Although the requirement that this should be sudden (**Duffy**) has been removed by the **2009 Act**, it would appear that she did not lose control at all. She had time to cool down before picking up the knife and stabbing her husband so arguably was in full control of her actions. Should she succeed in establishing a loss of control she would probably be able to rely on fear of violence as the qualifying trigger. Finally, she would need to convince a jury that a person of her age and sex, and in her circumstances (she had been abused by her husband) would have done the same, or similar. This may also be possible but due to the difficulty of proving the initial loss of control, she may be better off relying on the defence of diminished responsibility.

In **Dowds 2012**, in an appeal to the CA after the **2009 Act** came into force, D argued that acute intoxication was a recognised medical condition. He and his partner had a long history of drunkenness and violence, and both had been drinking when he attacked her with a knife and killed her. His appeal failed and the CA held that the new law was not intended to change the rule that voluntary intoxication was not capable of establishing diminished responsibility.

So, if D has a medical condition and is also drunk the jury should ignore the drink and just consider the medical condition (**Dietschmann**).

If the intoxication results from a medical condition, such as alcohol dependency syndrome, the jury can consider the drink but must ask whether it amounts to an abnormality (**Wood**).

The **Coroners and Justice Act 2009** does not change the rules on this (**Dowds**).

Exercise 11 application practice

In **Wood**, D had been diagnosed with 'alcohol dependency syndrome' and killed in a frenzied attack whilst drunk, having woken after a party to find a man attempting to have oral sex with him. Apply the new law to this case as I did for **Thornton** above.

Exercise 12 evaluation practice

Expand a little on the following sentences to produce an argument for or against the amended law. You may agree or disagree with the points made.

The removal of the need for a 'sudden and temporary' loss of control is an improvement.

The inclusion of a fear of serious violence as a qualifying trigger may be an improvement in cases where someone is reacting to violence but doesn't meet the requirements for the defence of self-defence.

Reference to a recognised medical condition is clearer than the old law on diminished responsibility, which was complex and hard for juries to understand.

Self-test questions

> *What are 'qualifying triggers' for loss of control under* **s 2** *of the* **Coroners and Justice Act 2009**?
>
> *What does the* **Act** *specifically exclude as a qualifying trigger?*
>
> *What does* **s 54(3)** *exclude when looking at the circumstances of D? Give an example.*
>
> *What type of evidence will be required for the defence of diminished responsibility?*
>
> *Who has the burden of proving this defence?*
>
> *What is excluded as a trigger under* **s 55**?
>
> *In which 2003 case was it held that if D is intoxicated and suffering from diminished responsibility the jury must ignore the intoxication?*
>
> *In which case, heard after the Act came into force, was the above point confirmed?*
>
> *When might intoxication support a defence and in which 1989 case was this established?*

Exercise 13 Examination practice

AQA January 2012

Despite some recent reforms, there are still criticisms to be made of the current law on murder and voluntary manslaughter. Consider relevant criticisms of that law, and suggest any reforms that may be appropriate. (25 marks)

A similar OCR question also for January 2012 in relation to voluntary manslaughter

Discuss the extent to which recent reforms to murder in the Coroners and Justice Act are a change for the better but have not necessarily satisfied those who campaigned for change (50 marks)

If intent cannot be proved then there is no *mens rea* for murder, and manslaughter will be the appropriate charge. There are two types, gross negligence manslaughter and unlawful act manslaughter.

Gross negligence manslaughter

In **Adomako**, an anaesthetist had failed to monitor a patient during an operation. The patient later died as a result. The doctor was accused of manslaughter.

The CA held that in order to prove gross negligence manslaughter there must be:

a risk of death

a duty of care

breach of that duty

gross negligence as regards that breach, which must be sufficient to justify criminal liability

Risk of death

The test was confirmed in **Misra 2004** (another case of medical negligence) where the CA stated that grossly negligent treatment, which exposed a patient to the risk of death, and caused death, would make the doctor liable for manslaughter. The CA also held that it had been 'clearly established' that a risk of death was needed; a risk of bodily injury or injury to health was not enough.

Duty, breach and gross negligence

Duty and breach are as for civil law. In **Wacker 2003**, the Ds were transporting about 60 illegal immigrants in a lorry. For some time during the journey there was no ventilation. Most of the immigrants died and the Ds were convicted of gross negligence manslaughter. The judge had referred to **Adomako** and the 'ordinary principles of the law of negligence'. They owed the people they were transporting a duty and had not acted as a reasonable person would, as they had not made sure there was ventilation, so they had breached that duty. The CA agreed that they had assumed a duty of care for the victims and rejected their appeal.

As regards what amounts to grossly negligent treatment, the jury must decide whether D's breach of duty was sufficiently grossly negligent to be deemed criminal.

In **Wood and Hodgson 2003**, a 10-year-old girl was visiting the Ds. She found some ecstasy tablets hidden in a cigarette packet and took some. She later died in hospital. They were charged with gross negligence manslaughter. Applying the rules:

Duty: they owed her a duty as a visitor and/or as a child in their care.

Breach: There was evidence that they had hidden the tablets, and that they had attempted to treat her, but they did not call an ambulance for some time. They had breached their duty to her by not taking reasonable care.

Gross negligence: However, the jury found that they had not shown a sufficiently high level of negligence to be deemed criminal.

Result: They were not guilty of gross negligence manslaughter.

Summary of the rules on gross negligence manslaughter from Adomako and Misra

There must be:

A risk of death

A duty of care

Breach of that duty

Gross negligence as regards that breach, which must be sufficient to justify criminal liability

Exercise 14 Case study on Evans

In **Evans (Gemma) 2009**, D supplied heroin to her 16-year-old half-sister, who injected it herself. When she showed symptoms of having overdosed neither D nor her mother attempted to get medical help; they merely put the girl to bed, and the next morning she was dead. D and her mother were charged with manslaughter and both were convicted. D appealed and argued she owed no duty.

Which type of manslaughter do you think she was charged with? Give reasons for your answer.

Which case(s) would you use to best illustrate your answer to Q1?

Which is the leading case on this type of manslaughter?

What are the main elements of this charge and in which case were they restated?

Using cases in support, apply the law to the given facts to come to a reasoned conclusion as to why it was decided that D was guilty of manslaughter, and whether you think her appeal is likely to succeed.

Unlawful act manslaughter

There are three separate issues to address in the *actus reus*

- **an unlawful act**
- **which is dangerous**
- **which causes death**

To be 'unlawful' the act must be a crime (**Lamb**) a civil wrong is not enough. Whether the unlawful act is dangerous is an objective test. It was stated in **Church 1967** that

> *"the unlawful act must be such as all sober and reasonable people would inevitably recognise must subject the other person to, at least, the risk of some harm resulting therefrom, albeit not serious harm"*

Physical assaults will usually be deemed dangerous, as in **R v M (J); R v M (S) 2012**, where two Ds were involved in a violent incident at a nightclub and one of the doormen collapsed from shock shortly afterwards and died. The CA held that sober and reasonable people would have recognised that the doormen were at the risk of some harm.

With crimes like robbery and burglary much will depend on the circumstances.

The In **Dawson** the robbery was not dangerous because V's heart condition was not obvious – reasonable people but would not see any risk of harm.

In **Watson** the burglary became dangerous once the man's frailty was obvious – reasonable people would see the risk of harm.

In **Bristow** the burglary was dangerous from the start because the risk was obvious to reasonable people at that stage

The unlawful act itself must cause the death. In **Cato 1976**, D supplied, and assisted V to take, heroin which resulted in death. It was held that he had unlawfully administered a drug which caused death and so was guilty of manslaughter. This can be compared to **Dalby 1982**, where the CA quashed the conviction because although D had supplied drugs (an unlawful act) this had not caused death. V had injected himself and this broke the chain of causation. After some doubt it was confirmed by the HL in **Kennedy 2007** that in the case of a fully informed adult self-administering the drug, it would never be appropriate to find the supplier guilty of manslaughter.

In **R v M (J); R v M (S) 2012**, two Ds were involved in a violent incident at a nightclub after being asked to leave. One of the doormen collapsed from shock shortly afterwards and died. The CA confirmed that it was not necessary for D to have foreseen any specific harm to the victim. What mattered was whether 'reasonable and sober people' would have recognised that the unlawful activities subjected the victim to the risk of harm. On the facts, it was clear that such people would have recognised that the doormen involved in the effort to control the Ds were at the risk of some harm.

Summary of unlawful act manslaughter

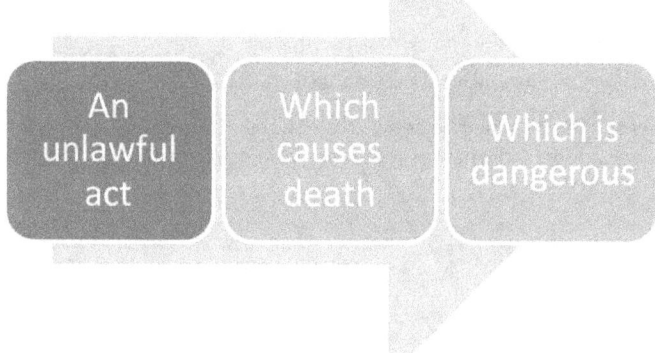

Exercise 15 Case study on Willoughby

In **Willoughby 2004**, D was the owner of a disused public house in Canterbury. He had recruited a local taxi driver to help him set fire to the building for financial purposes. They used petrol as an accelerant and an explosion occurred. The building collapsed and the taxi driver was killed. D was charged with, and convicted of, gross negligence manslaughter. On appeal, the CA said that it was "entirely unnecessary in this case to have recourse to the principles of manslaughter by gross negligence" and that the jury should have been directed in respect of unlawful act manslaughter. Adding that had they been so then, "a straightforward case of manslaughter, death having resulted from the unlawful and dangerous act of spreading petrol pursuant to a plan to set fire to the premises, would have been apparent".

What was D charged with?

What alternative charge was seen as more appropriate, and why?

Although Willoughby was charged with gross negligence manslaughter, the CA clearly thought a charge of unlawful act manslaughter was more appropriate. Apply the law on this offence to the given facts.

Examination tip

Look for clues in the scenario. If there is an unlawful act such as an assault then unlawful act manslaughter is likely to be most appropriate. If there is a lawful action that seems negligent then discuss gross negligence manslaughter. The CA in **Adomako** suggested that it could be gross negligence manslaughter where, e.g., an electrician caused a death by faulty wiring. This was *obiter dicta* but could be referred to if the given scenario involved such circumstances, or something similar. The two types of manslaughter overlap so you may need to discuss both. If you think it is constructive manslaughter, discuss this first, but if, e.g., there is doubt as to whether there is an act or omission, or whether the act is unlawful, go on to gross negligence manslaughter as an alternative. If, as in **Willoughby**, there is some doubt as to whether a duty is owed, you could start with gross negligence manslaughter and go on to constructive manslaughter as an alternative.

Exercise 16

The following cases were looked at with murder but as no intent was proved, the result is manslaughter. State which type of manslaughter would be most appropriate, and why, and explain how the rules on causation apply.

Hancock and Shankland

Stone & Dobinson

Nedrick

Exercise 17 application practice

Look at the following brief scenarios. Explain whether you will face a manslaughter charge, which type and why.

You are angry and wave your fist at Cathy. She is of a very nervous disposition and dies of fright.

You are angry and throw a brick at Kate, which misses. She is of a very nervous disposition and dies of fright.

You are taking the neighbour's five-year-old daughter to school when you bump into a friend. You tell the girl to go on alone and on the way she is run over and dies.

You accidently start a fire in the school cellar. You don't want to get into trouble so you run away and leave it burning. The caretaker is overcome by smoke and dies.

Self-test questions

> *What are the elements required to prove gross negligence manslaughter?*

> *Can you commit either type of manslaughter by omission?*

> *What were the facts and principle in **Church**?*

> *What is the difference between **Cato** and **Dalby**?*

> *What did the HL decide in **Kennedy (2007)**?*

Examination practice

There is no evaluation needed for involuntary manslaughter, so no essay question. We haven't covered defences yet so it is too early for an application question. The examination questions in Chapter 6 cover involuntary manslaughter along with various other offences, and also defences.

For a range of free interactive exercises please go to www.drsr.org and click on 'Free Exercises' to see what's available.

Assault and battery at common law

Two separate offences, assault and battery, come under the term 'common assault' because they come from the common law and are not defined in any statute. The **Criminal Justice Act 1988 s 39** classifies them as summary offences so for convenience they are charged under this section.

The definition of assault used by the CA in **Ireland 1996** is 'an act by which a person intentionally or recklessly causes another to apprehend immediate and unlawful violence'. Thus assault needs no physical contact; it is enough that someone is in fear of such contact. Words may negate an assault by suggesting there will be no harm under certain conditions (**Turbeville**).

Battery requires contact (the application of force) but this can be very slight, and even to touch someone's clothes can be battery, as decided in **Thomas**.

The force must be unlawful; consent may make touching lawful and so remove *actus reus* (e.g., in sports).

Force may be indirect. In **DPP v K 1990**, a schoolboy put acid in a hot air drier and this was held to be a battery on the boy who was burned by it. In **Haystead 2000**, D punched his girlfriend and she dropped her baby, this was held to be a battery on the baby.

Summary of assault and battery

Assault *Actus reus*	
to cause the victim to apprehend	What is the effect on the victim?
immediate and unlawful personal violence	Ireland
Words may be enough, or even silence	Wilson/Ireland
Mens rea	intent to cause the victim to apprehend immediate and unlawful personal violence or being subjectively reckless as to this
Battery *Actus reus*	
unlawful application of force to another	Collins v Wilcock
Can include touching V's clothes	Thomas
May include indirect force	DPP v K
Mens rea	intent to apply unlawful force or being subjectively reckless as to this

Assault occasioning actual bodily harm under s 47 Offences against the Person Act 1861(ABH)

For ABH there must first be an assault (assault or battery). This assault must cause (occasion) some bodily harm (not trivial harm).

In **Savage1991**, a girl threw a glass of beer over another girl. As she did so, she let go of the glass which broke, resulting in a cut to the other girl's wrist. There was no proof she intended to throw the glass and she said it was an accident. However, she did intend to throw the beer. The throwing of the beer was enough for the *actus reus* of battery. She intended to do this, so there was *mens rea* too. Once battery was proved, for her to be convicted under **s 47** the prosecution merely had to show the battery had 'occasioned' (caused) the harm, i.e., it made a significant contribution to the harm and the chain of causation was not broken. This confirmed **Roberts**, that once there is *mens rea* for an assault or battery no further mental state has to be established, only the extra *actus reus* of causing harm. Think about it as an equation:

Assault (AR + MR of assault or battery) + occasions (AR) + harm (AR) = **s 47**

As regards harm, in **Miller 1954**, this was held to be any hurt or injury calculated to 'interfere with health or comfort', which could include mental discomfort. In **Chan-Fook 1994**, the CA qualified this a little and held that really trivial or insignificant harm is excluded. Psychiatric injury was said to suffice but not "mere emotions" such as fear, distress or panic.

Summary of s 47 ABH

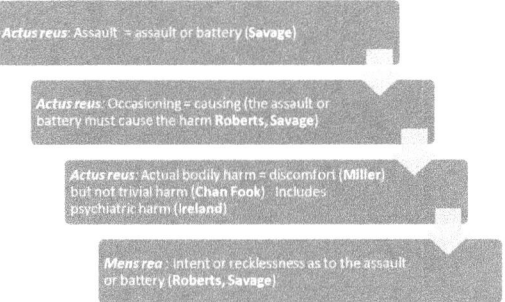

Actus reus: Assault = assault or battery (**Savage**)

Actus reus: Occasioning = causing (the assault or battery must cause the harm **Roberts, Savage**)

Actus reus: Actual bodily harm = discomfort (**Miller**) but not trivial harm (**Chan Fook**) Includes psychiatric harm (**Ireland**)

Mens rea: Intent or recklessness as to the assault or battery (**Roberts, Savage**)

Exercise 18 Case study Ross Smith

In **DPP v Ross Smith 2006**, D held his ex-girlfriend down and cut off her ponytail with a pair of kitchen scissors. At trial the magistrates acquitted D of **s 47** ABH on the basis that although there was an assault (battery) she had not suffered physical or psychological harm. The QBD disagreed. Referring to **Chan-Fook** and **Burstow** the court held that 'harm' included hurt or damage and 'actual' meant merely that it was not trivial harm. The court also held that pain was not a necessary requirement of actual bodily harm. Even though technically hair is merely dead tissue, Judge P said that while it is attached to the body "it falls within the meaning of 'bodily' in the phrase 'actual bodily harm'. It is concerned with the body of the individual victim".

What was Smith charged with at the Magistrates' court?

Which other charge might have been more successful? Give reasons and/or cases in support

What was the main reason that Judge P gave for finding the cutting of hair to be 'bodily' harm?

In which case was it decided that actual bodily harm includes any hurt or injury that interferes with the health or comfort of the victim?

In which case was this description modified to include psychiatric injury but not "mere emotions" such as fear, distress or panic?

Apply the law on ABH to the given facts so show whether you think he should be guilty of ABH or battery.

Wounding and grievous bodily harm under s 18 & 20 *Offences against the Person Act 1861 (GBH)*

These two offences are commonly called malicious wounding (**s 20**) and wounding with intent (**s 18**).

There is very little difference in the *actus reus*; each needs either a wound (**Eisenhower**) or serious injury (**Saunders**). In the joint appeals of **Ireland & Burstow**, the HL said psychiatric harm could amount to GBH.

Examination tip

Look for clues in the scenario as to whether to discuss **s 18**, **s 20** or both. If there is a cut, discuss wounding under either **s 18** or **s 20**, depending on *mens rea*. If it is only a small cut also discuss **s 47**. If there is a serious internal injury (fracture; internal bleeding; broken ribs), discuss GBH. It was confirmed in Savage that a jury could bring in **s 20** as an alternative verdict when someone is charged under **s 18**, and **s 47** as an alternative to **s 20**. Finally, although it doesn't matter how D inflicts or causes the harm, the use of a weapon may help in establishing intent to cause serious harm, and so point you to **s 18**.

Serious harm is usually required for GBH, but note should be taken of **Bollom 2004**. A baby suffered bruising to several parts of her body and her mother's partner was charged with GBH. Although the CA substituted the conviction for one of ABH, it was made clear that bruising could amount to GBH if the victim was a young child.

Examination tip

Bollom indicates that the age of the victim may be relevant in deciding the appropriate charge. This argument could also be applied to an old or vulnerable person so **Bollom** could be used to support a charge of **s 20** or **18** where if V was a more robust person it would be **s 47**.

Mens rea for **s 20** is intent or subjective recklessness. Importantly, D need not intend or recognise the risk of *serious* harm, only *some* harm. This was confirmed by the CA in **Mowatt 1968** and later approved by the HL in **Parmenter 1992**.

The *mens rea* for **s 18** is specific intent, i.e., intent only. It was confirmed in **Belfon**, where D had slashed someone with a razor, that recklessness was not enough, there must be intent to cause serious harm. This was confirmed in **Parmenter** and makes **s 18** a much more serious offence.

A further difference with **s 18** *mens rea* is that it includes intent to resist or prevent a lawful arrest. This is seen in **Morrison 1989** where D dived through a window resisting arrest and a police officer was badly cut. The CA upheld his conviction and held that it was enough that he intended resisting arrest even though he did not intend to cause her serious harm. He intended to resist arrest and was reckless as to the harm (as he dragged her with him) and this was enough.

Summary of s 18 and s 20

Actus reus	
Inflict or cause	Mean the same thing (Ireland)
Wound	Open cut (Eisenhower)
Grievous bodily harm	Serious harm (Smith/Saunders)
Mens rea	
S 20 Intent or recklessness	To cause some harm (Mowatt)
S 18 Intent only	To cause serious harm (Parmenter)

Exercise 19 Case study on GBH

In **Horsley (unreported) January 2010**, D had poured bleach over a woman who had asked staff to tell him and his friends to be quiet during a Harry Potter film. After leaving the cinema he saw her go into a restaurant with her family and shouted abuse at her. He then went to a garage and bought a bottle of bleach. He went back to the restaurant and squirted the bleach over her head. Although prompt attention prevented her from suffering serious burns, her hair had turned white and she said she was mentally scarred by the incident and had trouble sleeping. He pleaded guilty to ABH but denied the more serious charge of causing GBH with intent.

Using your knowledge of the non-fatal offences explain which offence under the Offences against the Person Act you think the jury convicted him of.

Exercise 20

Note which case the following principles came from, with a brief explanation

An assault can be negated by words.

Words can be enough for an assault (two 1997 cases).

Silence can be enough for an assault (1983 and/or 1997 case).

A battery can be indirect (1990 case).

Mere emotions such as fear, distress or panic are not enough for actual bodily harm.

A foreseeable action by the victim will not break the chain of causation.

D does not need *mens rea* for the harm, only the assault.

Grievous means serious harm.

Wound means an open cut.

The HL confirmed that psychiatric harm can come under **s 47**, **18** or **20** (a 1997 joint appeal).

Examination tips for all the non-fatal offences

Choose the appropriate offence carefully. **S 47** ABH covers a wide area and students are often tempted to discuss this offence alone when there has been a serious injury, or a weapon has been used. On the other hand, although even a small cut could technically be a wound, it is more appropriate to charge such an injury as ABH, especially if not done with intent. You don't want to use precious time discussing an inappropriate offence but if you fail to deal with the most suitable one you will limit your marks. If you are unsure, deal with you first choice in detail and then briefly discuss the alternative. (Remember that **Savage** confirms that a jury can bring in **s 20** as an alternative verdict to **s 18**, and **s 47** as an alternative to **s 20**, so you could use this to support why you have chosen a higher charge). Assault or battery may be the appropriate charge even if harm occurs if there is a causation issue – if the assault did not cause the harm it won't be ABH (this argument was raised in **Roberts** but failed as her actions were foreseeable). There is usually a hint in exam scenarios to point you towards a particular offence. The following exercise should help you to recognise which charge would be most appropriate.

Exercise 21 Application practice

Look at the phrases below and say which offence and any particular issues that they suggest to you and why, adding cases where possible.

Goran pulled at Lisa's jacket and she fell over, grazing her knee

Tracey threw a book at Sam who jumped aside and pushed over an elderly woman, who cried out in pain

The woman had brittle bones and broke her leg when she fell

Tom sent a text message to Ahmed saying he will beat him next time he sees him

Pete lashed out at Ben with a knife, cutting his cheek

Problems and reforms

The Law Commission has been considering codification of the criminal law for some time. This was a huge task and so it was decided it would be better to work on a series of self-contained bills to deal with different parts of the criminal law. In 1993 the Commission produced a report (No 218) and draft Bill on the non-fatal offences against the person. This never received parliamentary time but in 1998 the government produced its own Bill incorporating most of the recommended changes, but again little happened.

The Law Commission is due to produce a further paper in late 2013.

The Commission notes that the Act is widely recognised as being outdated and that it uses archaic language. It also says that the structure of the Act is unsatisfactory; because there is no clear hierarchy of offences and the differences between **sections 18, 20** and **47** are not clearly spelt out.

The following is a quote from their website in 2012:

> *"Section 20 (maliciously wounding or inflicting grievous bodily harm) is seen as more serious than section 47 (assault occasioning actual bodily harm) but the maximum penalty (five years) is the same. Furthermore the* actus reus *for sections 18 (intentionally wounding or causing grievous bodily harm) and 20 appear to be the same apart from the distinction between "causing" and "inflicting", which is notoriously difficult to draw.*
>
> *This project will therefore aim to restructure the law on offences against the person, probably by creating a structured hierarchy of offences, as well as modernising and simplifying the language by which these offences are defined".*

The table below shows the proposals from the 1998 Bill. The offences are redefined and in all of them the *mens rea* matches the *actus reus*. The Law Commission project commencing in 2013 is likely to result in something very similar, although we cannot be sure at this stage.

Name of proposed offence	Explanation of proposed offence	Current offence

Intentional serious injury	Clause 1: intentionally causing serious injury	**S 18**
Reckless serious injury	Clause 2: recklessly causing serious injury	**S 20**
Intentional or reckless injury	Clause 3: intentionally or recklessly causing injury	**S 47**
Assault	Clause 4: intentionally or recklessly applying force to or causing an impact on the body of another; or intentionally or recklessly causing another to believe force is imminent	Common assault (assault and battery)

Exercise 22 Evaluation practice

A critique of the law should include any positive developments as well as any proposals for reform where these apply. The following list gives a negative point about the non-fatal offences. Add a comment with something positive or with a proposed reform of the area.

Assault and battery are still not included in statute law but left to judicial reasoning alone

The word assault is ambiguous, it means the specific offence of causing someone to apprehend immediate personal violence (**Ireland**) but also means both an assault and a battery for the purpose of finding an 'assault' which occasions harm for **s 47**

The vocabulary in the **1861 Act** is out-dated and unclear. Words such as 'whosoever' 'occasioning' 'grievous' and 'maliciously' are not in common use today and may anyway have meant something different in 1861 when the Act was written

The structure of the offences is illogical, as are the section numbers. This is partly because the Act was a consolidated one drawing from several sources, but it means that the distinction between the offences is unclear

It seems harsh that for ABH no *mens rea* is required for the harm caused, only for the assault or battery (**Savage**)

The meaning of 'immediate' in assault (and ABH) is vague

The sentencing maximums for **s 47** and **s 20** seem illogical as both sections carry the same maximum but they are very different offences

The different wording of **s 18** and **20**, with 'causing' in the former and 'inflicting' in the latter, is misleading

S 18 & **20** contain 4 different offences, reckless GBH, reckless wounding, GBH with intent and wounding with intent, which is confusing

A wound can be any cut (**Eisenhower**) which means that technically a small cut could amount to a wound under **s 18** or **20**

It seems harsh that no *mens rea* is required for serious harm under **s 20**, only for some harm (**Mowatt**)

It seems harsh that if D is resisting arrest there can be a charge under **s 18** when the *mens rea* as regards the harm caused is only recklessness, not intent (**Morrison**)

Self-test questions

Why is causation important in a case of ABH?

According to Roberts, what sort of action by V could break the chain of causation?

How has 'wound' been interpreted and in which case?

How has 'grievous bodily harm' been interpreted and in which case?

What is the difference in the mens rea between **s 20** and **s 18**?

Exercise 23 Examination practice

AQA June 2011

The non-fatal offences against the person have been subjected to frequent criticism. Explain and discuss these criticisms, and suggest what reforms might be desirable. (25 marks)

A similar OCR question for June 2012

The Offences against the Persons Act has outlived its usefulness; it should be reformed as soon as possible.

Discuss the extent to which this statement is accurate (50 marks)

For a range of free interactive exercises please go to www.drsr.org and click on 'Free Exercises' to see what's available.

Insanity

There are two main propositions of law called the **M'Naghten** rules.

Firstly, everyone is to be presumed to be sane until proved otherwise.

Secondly, insanity may be proved if, at the time of committing the act, D was

> *"labouring under such a defect of reason, from disease of the mind, as not to know the nature and quality of the act he was doing, or if he did know it, that he did not know he was doing what was wrong."*

Disease of the mind

In **Bratty v A-G for Northern Ireland 1963**, Lord Denning said a disease of the mind was

> *"any mental disorder which has manifested itself in violence and is prone to recur"*

This indicates something more than a temporary lapse but in **Smith (Mark) 2012**, D was violent and abusive while travelling on an aircraft and had to be restrained by cabin staff. Medical evidence was that he had a brief reactive psychosis characterised by delusions and hallucinations but the defence was held to be insanity even though the psychosis was 'brief'.

Defect of reason

The disease of the mind must cause the defect of reason. The courts make a distinction between internal factors and external factors. If the 'defect of reason' is caused by an internal factor, a disease, this points to insanity. If it is caused by an external factor, like a blow to the head and concussion, then it is likely to be automatism. Some cases involving diabetics have shown the problems with this distinction. In **Quick**, D had killed after taking insulin and then failing to eat. In **Hennessey**, D had killed after failing to take insulin. Look at the diagram – on which side would **Quick** be and on which side would **Hennessy** be?

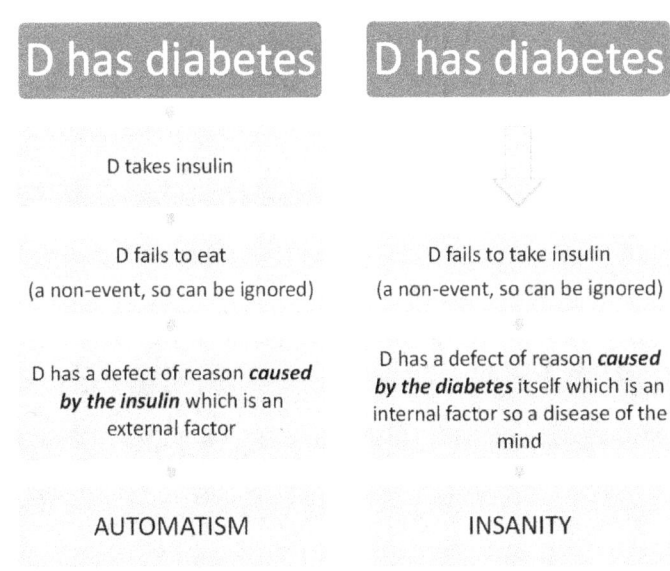

Did you get it right?

Quick would be on the left as he had taken insulin and this caused the defect – an external factor. Hennessey would be on the right because the disease itself caused his defect – an internal factor.

Even if there is a disease of the mind, it is only insanity if D did not know the nature and quality of the act and did not know that it was wrong.

D did not know the nature and quality of the act

In **Burgess**, the fact that he was sleepwalking meant he did not know the nature of his actions. Similarly, in **Sullivan** and **Hennessy**, they were not aware of what they were doing at the time.

Did not know he was doing what was wrong

This means D did not know the act was legally wrong. In **Windle 1952**, D killed his wife with an overdose of aspirin. There was evidence of mental illness but on giving himself up he said 'I suppose they will hang me for this' thereby indicating he knew that what he had done was legally wrong. It is not a matter of whether D believes it was morally right or wrong.

Example

Mike obeys voices telling him to kill prostitutes because they are immoral. If he knows killing is legally wrong he cannot rely on the defence, even though he believes it to be morally right.

In **Johnson 2007**, D forced his way into a neighbour's flat and, for no apparent reason, stabbed him with a large kitchen knife. There was evidence that D suffered from paranoid schizophrenia and he said that he did not know what he was doing. Following **Windle**, the CA held that even if there was evidence of a disease of the mind, if he knew that what he did was legally wrong there was no issue of insanity to be left to the jury.

Insanity and intoxication

If the defect of reason comes about through intoxication, the insanity defence fails. In **Lipman**, D had taken LSD and had a hallucination in which he thought he was fighting snakes. He killed his girlfriend by stuffing a sheet down her throat. He did not know the nature or quality of his act but, as the LSD was voluntarily taken, the defence failed. If the defect comes from alcoholism, it could succeed as this can be classed as a 'disease'.

Automatism

The defence of automatism arises where D's act was 'automatic' and so was not voluntary. Thus, it is negating *actus reus* rather than *mens rea*. A successful plea of automatism leads to a complete acquittal so it would be preferred to pleading insanity.

For the defence to succeed it must be shown that:

the act was involuntary

this was due to an external factor

In **Bratty v Attorney General for N I (1963)** Lord Denning said

> *"... automatism means an act which is done by the muscles without any control by the mind such as a spasm, a reflex action or a convulsion or an act done by a person who is not conscious of what he is doing ..."*

The lack of control must be total. In **Attorney-General's Reference (No 2 of 1992) 1994**, D killed two people when his lorry crashed into a car on the hard shoulder of the motorway. He pleaded automatism on the grounds that driving for so long on a motorway had resulted in a 'trance-like' state and he was suffering from what is called 'driving without awareness'. On referral to the CA, it was held that this did not amount to automatism because his lack of awareness was not total. This confirmed **Broome v Perkins 1987**, where a diabetic, suffering from hypoglycaemia, hit another car. It was held that, as D was able to exercise some control, automatism was not available.

The essence of automatism is that the crime was the result of an external factor causing an involuntary act on the part of D. As we saw with insanity, the distinction the courts make between internal and external has produced some fairly bizarre cases. The LC said in its 2012 paper that the "line drawn between sane and insane automatism can never make medical sense".

External factors would include prescribed drugs, such as the insulin in **Quick**. In **Hill v Baxter 1958**, a hypothetical example was given of D being attacked by a swarm of bees whilst driving a car. If this caused a total loss of control, the automatism defence would succeed.

Examination tip

The defences of insanity and automatism are closely linked so you may need to discuss both. Look for whether the cause of D's actions is internal or external, but remember that the automatism defence would be better as it results in an acquittal.

Automatism and intoxication

As D must be acting involuntarily, the defence cannot be relied upon if the automatism was self-induced, e.g., by drinking or taking drugs, as in **Lipman**. Prescribed drugs would be OK and in **Hardie** the court accepted the defence where the drugs were not prescribed to D but he had expected them to calm him down so the effects were unpredictable.

Summary of insanity and automatism

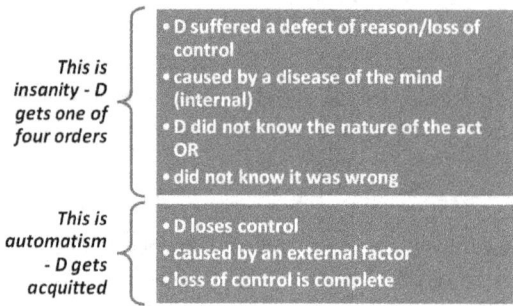

This is insanity - D gets one of four orders
- D suffered a defect of reason/loss of control
- caused by a disease of the mind (internal)
- D did not know the nature of the act OR
- did not know it was wrong

This is automatism - D gets acquitted
- D loses control
- caused by an external factor
- loss of control is complete

Exercise 24

The Law Commission published a scoping paper in 2012. The introduction to the proposed project is on the Law Commission website. Click on the link below and look at what they say, then answer the questions.

http://www.justice.gov.uk/lawcommission/areas/insanity.htm

What question does the Law Commission say is posed by the defence of insanity?

At what time is D's mental condition relevant for the defence of insanity to apply?

What, according to the Law Commission, amounts to the defence of 'sane automatism'?

The Law Commission states that the rules on insanity date from 1843. From which case did the rules come?

What does the Law Commission say is not clear about the defence of insanity?

According to the Law Commission is the defence used often?

Give a reason for your previous answer.

What problem is seen as regards evidence from medical professionals?

What does the Law Commission say as regards the term 'insane' in describing those with a mental illness?

What does the Law Commission say as regards the term 'insane' in describing those with learning disabilities, learning difficulties, or epilepsy?

Can you give a case example of when epilepsy was classed as insanity?

What does the Law Commission say is the problem with the case law on these two defences?

What other potential problem is highlighted?

Intoxication

Intoxication can be by drink, drugs or solvents and may be voluntary or involuntary. It overlaps with the other defences, as discussed above with automatism and insanity. With self-defence, an intoxicated mistake cannot be relied on to justify using force in self-defence.

The rules on involuntary intoxication come from **Kingston**. The essential point is to find if D had *mens rea* despite the intoxication. If so the defence will fail. A drunken intent is still intent.

The rules on voluntary intoxication are more complex. The case of **Majewski** made the distinction between a specific intent crime and a basic intent crime. Although the reasoning was not fully clear, and some confusion arose in **Heard 2007**, the distinction is usually interpreted as specific intent being crimes where the *mens rea* is intent only (e.g., murder and theft) and basic intent being crimes where the *mens rea* includes recklessness.

In **Heard 2007**, the CA decided that that not all offences could be categorised as basic or specific offences as some had elements of both.

Examination tip

When explaining specific and basic intent use the commonly accepted **Majewski** rule and briefly mention that it is not fully clear following **Heard**. The main thing is to make sure you explain that if intoxication succeeds as a defence to a specific intent crime, D will still be guilty of any related basic intent crime e.g., murder – manslaughter, **s 18 – s 20**.

The 'Dutch Courage' rule

In **Attorney General for Northern Ireland v Gallagher 1963**, D decided to kill his wife. He bought a knife and a bottle of whisky. He drank the whisky and then stabbed her and pleaded intoxication as a defence. The HL held that once a person formed an intention to kill then the defence would fail. This is called the 'Dutch Courage' rule.

Summary of intoxication

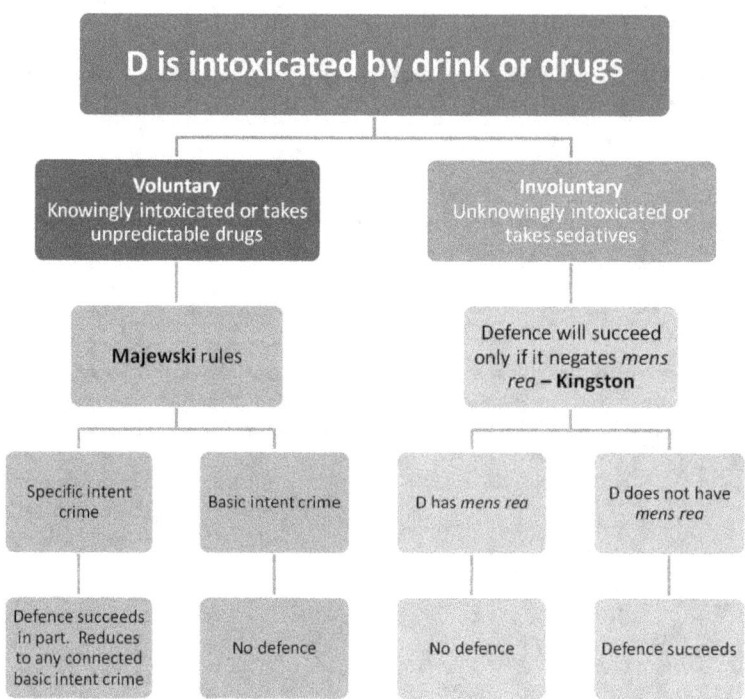

Exercise 25 Marison case study (insanity, automatism and intoxication)

In **Marison 1996**, D was a diabetic who was charged with causing death by dangerous driving. He lost control of his car after losing consciousness, and crashed into another car, killing the other driver. He had had several episodes of losing consciousness prior to this event, during one of which he had also lost control of his car. The court held that he could not rely on the defence of automatism because he had driven in the knowledge that such an incident could occur. Even if he had been in a state of automatism at the time of the actual crash, he had been driving until then with the knowledge that he could lose consciousness which made an accident foreseeable. His actions were reckless, he had therefore been driving dangerously before the crash, at which time there was no automatism present; he was in control.

What is needed for the automatism defence to succeed and why did it fail in this case?

In which other driving case did a diabetic fail in this defence, and why?

The fact that he was driving knowing of the possibility of losing consciousness was reckless and can be seen as self-induced automatism. This is similar to voluntary intoxication. In which case was it said that taking drink or drugs was reckless in itself, and so provided *mens rea*?

When might the intoxication defence succeed even if D is reckless? Give a case in support.

What was the point made in **Hardie** that meant the automatism defence could succeed?

In **Hardie**, why was D found not to be reckless?

Which defence could have succeeded in **Marison**?

In a case like **Hardie,** will it matter whether it is a specific or basic intent crime?

What effect, if any, will voluntary intoxication have on the defences of insanity and automatism?

Consent

Express consent is where a person expressly allows the action, but to succeed as a defence it must be real, or informed, consent. In **Tabassum 2000**, D had persuaded several women to allow him to measure their breasts. He told them that it was for producing a database for doctors. The women consented to him doing this and were fully aware of the nature of the action he planned to take. However, they said that they only consented because they thought that D was a doctor with medical training. The CA agreed with the trial judge that consent to a medical examination was not the same as consent to indecent behaviour. The act consented to was not the act done.

This decision is perhaps to be preferred to **Richardson 1999**, where the CA allowed the defence even though the patients only consented because they did not know the full facts, i.e., that he had been suspended.

Consent may also be implied e.g., in sporting situations. Some examples of when consent could be implied were set out by the CA in **A-G's Reference (No 6 of 1980) 1981**. The CA said it was not in the public interest that people should cause each other actual bodily harm for no good reason but that implied consent would occur in "properly conducted games and sports, lawful chastisement or correction, reasonable surgical interference, dangerous exhibitions, etc." What is termed 'rough horseplay' has also been accepted as implying consent, as in **Aitken** and **Jones**.

In **Barnes 2004**, D had been found guilty of grievous bodily harm after a late tackle in a football match. His conviction was quashed and the CA held that criminal prosecutions should be reserved for conduct which was 'sufficiently grave' to be classed as criminal.

Consent is mainly relevant to the non-fatal offences against the person.

In most cases it makes the action lawful, so no offence occurs, as in sports cases such as **Barnes 2004**. This means it can be used to deny the *actus reus* of the offence rather than as a defence.

Examination tip

In an examination you would be given credit for either approach. You could say Barnes can use the defence of consent if charged with GBH. This is so even though **Brown** & **Dica** suggest you cannot consent to intentional serious harm, because it is a sporting situation. Alternatively, as part of the *actus reus* of GBH is that it is done 'unlawfully', you can say that Barnes did not have the *actus reus* of the offence because the implied consent made his actions lawful. The same would apply to assault or battery as this is applying or causing V to apprehend 'unlawful' force, and to ABH because it is based on a prior assault if the *actus reus* is not complete there is no offence.

A final point, you can never consent to murder – **Pretty**.

Exercise 26 Consent

Choose a case from the list to match to the principle

Consent is never a defence to murder

Consent must be true consent, so a child may not be deemed to have consented

Consent can make even serious violence in sports lawful

There must be consent to harm, not just to sex

The CA set out some examples of when consent could be implied

Consent may be a valid defence even for serious harm if it is seen as 'rough horseplay'

Aitken

Dica

Barnes

A-G's Reference (No 6 of 1980)

Pretty

Burrell & Harmer

Summary of Consent

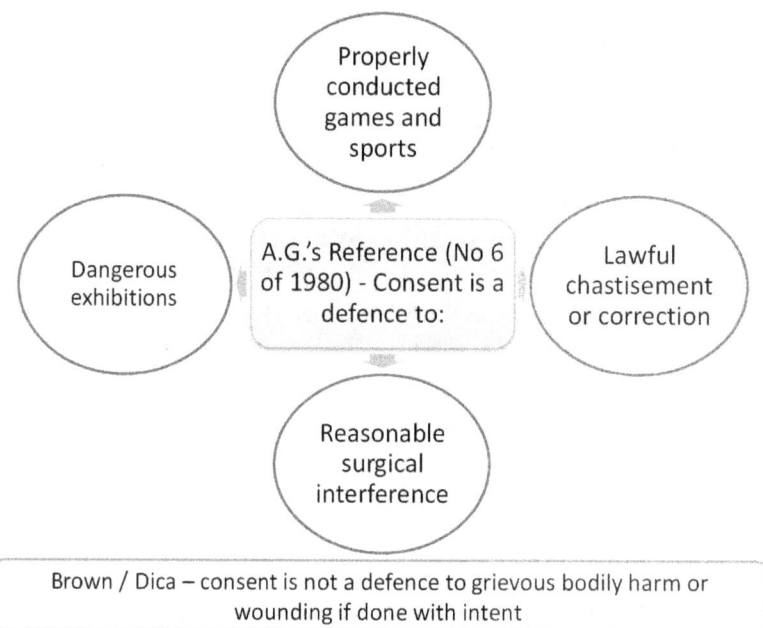

Brown / Dica – consent is not a defence to grievous bodily harm or wounding if done with intent

Self-defence and prevention of a crime

The defence of prevention of a crime comes from **s 3(1)** of the **Criminal Law Act 1967**, which states:

"A person may use such force as is reasonable in the circumstances in the prevention of crime"

Self-defence

Self-defence is a common law defence and includes defence of another. It is most often used as a defence against a charge of one of the non-fatal offences against the person. There are two main questions to consider:

did D honestly believe the action was justified? (what D thought; a subjective question)

was the degree of force reasonable in the circumstances? (what a reasonable person would do; an objective question).

In **Martin**, a farmer shot and killed a burglar and seriously injured another. According to evidence, they were retreating and posing no threat. The defence failed because the jury thought that using a pump-action shotgun was not reasonable in the circumstances.

The common law has now been partly put into statute. **S 76 Criminal Justice and Immigration Act 2008** adds to the common law on self-defence but does not replace it. In **Hitchins 2011**, the CA held that there was no difference between self-defence under the common law and **s 3**. **S 76** applies to both.

S 76(3) provides that whether the force is reasonable is decided by reference to the circumstances as D believed them to be.

If D mistakenly believes someone is being attacked or threatened, then self-defence may be relied on, even if there was no actual threat. This confirms **Williams (Gladstone) 1987**. A man saw a woman being robbed by a youth and struggled with him. D came on the scene and believed the youth to be under attack. He punched the man and was charged with actual bodily harm. His defence succeeded. The court held that he was to be judged on the facts as he saw them, even though he was mistaken.

S 76(4) provides that if D claims to have held a particular belief as regards the circumstances the reasonableness of that belief will be relevant as to whether D genuinely held it, but if D did genuinely hold it, D is entitled to rely on it whether or not it was mistaken, or (if it was mistaken) whether or not the mistake was a reasonable one to have made. This is also based on **Williams** and essentially means that although the mistake does not have to reasonable, if it is not reasonable the jury may not be convinced that it was genuinely held.

S 76(7((a) confirms what the court held in **Palmer 1971**, that D

"may not be able to weigh to a nicety the exact measure of any necessary action"

S 76(7((b) provides that if D only did what was "honestly and instinctively thought" to be necessary this would be "strong evidence that only reasonable action was taken".

Should D retreat?

In **McInnes 1971**, the CA said that a person is not obliged to retreat from a threat in order to rely on the defence, but it will be evidence for the jury when considering whether force was necessary, and if so whether it was reasonable. This is still the case; however, **s 76(6)** provides that the degree of force is not to be regarded as reasonable if it was disproportionate in the circumstances as D believed them to be. If leaving the scene is an easy option then it may mean any force used isn't seen as reasonable.

Self-defence and intoxication

S 76(5) provides that D cannot rely on any mistaken belief attributable to intoxication that was voluntarily induced.

In **O'Grady**, D hit his friend over the head in the mistaken belief that the friend was trying to kill him. His defence failed because his mistake was made because he was drunk. His belief may have been genuine, but the CA said he could not rely on a drunken mistake to justify his actions. **S 76(5)** confirms this.

Summary of Self-defence

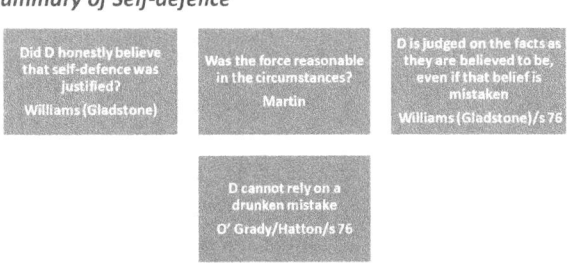

Exercise 27 Self-defence Case study on Hargreaves

In **Hargreaves 2010**, D was in a taxi with her boyfriend and another man, all of whom had been drinking. She was in the back and was having an argument with her boyfriend, who was sitting in the front. He turned towards her and she kicked out at him, ramming a stiletto heel through his eye and into his brain. She was charged with both grievous bodily harm with intent, and an alternative charge of inflicting grievous bodily harm. She said that she had kicked out at him as she believed he was going to attack her and pleaded self-defence. The judge said to the jury "There is no evidence to lead you to the conclusion the defendant was not acting in instinctive, reasonable self-defence." The defence succeeded and she was acquitted of both offences.

What was Ms Hargreaves charged with?

Under which sections of which Act do these offences arise?

What defence did she plead and what did the judge rule?

What are the requirements for this defence?

Must D retreat if possible? Use a case to support your answer.

Apply the law to the given facts to decide why the judge ruled as he did.

Do you see any problem with the fact that she succeeded in this defence?

Exercise 28 Application practice

In each of the following cases the person has gone on to cause someone's death. If charged with manslaughter, which defence do the phrases suggest you should discuss? Mention any specific issues you think they raise, with relevant cases, and what the effect will be for D.

Hari was convinced that everyone was plotting against him, and he ...

Irena was a diabetic who had taken her insulin, but had not eaten regularly and during a fit she ...

An owl flew into Dan's windscreen causing him to swerve and ...

Ahmed had been suffering from powerful delusions, but the drugs his doctor gave him caused an unusual reaction and ...

Max had never been the same since he was hit on the head and suffered concussion, he ...

Tom was a diabetic who had not taken his insulin and during a fit he ...

Imran had been driving so long he was in a semi-catatonic state and said he remembered nothing about the crash ...

Arnie had been hearing voices which told him all unbelievers must die so he ...

In the next few situations a different crime has been committed in each (shown in brackets). Explain what defence springs to mind and any issues that may be relevant, with cases where possible.

Henri was sent off for foul play (GBH **s 20**)

Jack thought he was being attacked and lashed out (battery)

Rula got an infection after Tom gave her nose piercings (ABH)

As he came out of the night club Ben saw a man approach and lashed out (ABH)

After taking several different drugs given to him by a friend Stefan went home to his girlfriend. In his confused state he totally flipped when she ran to hug him and thought she was a bear. He grabbed a knife and stabbed her (wounding with intent **s 18**)

Mira begged the doctor to give her an injection to end her life (murder)

Exercise 29 Evaluation practice

There are five defences and you will only need to discuss two of them so choose two and make a list of any problems, adding any areas where the law has improved through statutory or judicial intervention. Then add any proposals for reform which have not yet occurred.

Self-test questions

> *From which case do the insanity rules come?*
>
> *Is it insanity or automatism when the cause is external?*
>
> *What is 'Dutch courage' and will it provide a defence?*
>
> *If D successfully pleads intoxication to a specific intent crime such as murder what is the result?*
>
> *State two of the activities where consent is implied as stated in **A.G.'s Reference**.*
>
> *Why was the conviction quashed in **Barnes 2004**?*
>
> *Why was self-defence rejected by the jury in **Martin**?*
>
> *What was decided in Hatton and confirmed by **s 76**?*

Exercise 30 Examination practice January 2011

Write a critical analysis of any two of the general defences (insanity, automatism, intoxication, consent, self-defence/prevention of crime). Include in your answer a consideration of any proposals for reform of one of your chosen defences. (25 marks)

You will always only need to discuss two defences so pick those you feel most comfortable with and know them well.

A similar question for OCR for June 2012

Discuss the view that the defences of sane and insane automatism are in need of reform if they are to be of use in the modern English legal system (50 marks)

For a range of free interactive exercises please go to www.drsr.org and click on 'Free Exercises' to see what's available.

Revision 6 Examination practice

Here are two quick guides as a base for approaching problem questions. The first is on the assaults and the second on homicide. In each case you should apply the law as you go along, referring to the facts of the given scenario.

Assaults – working through a problem

Identify the offence or offences. Define them and explain the AR/MR as you work through the facts given. Only discuss relevant offences, don't try to cover them all. Note that for **s 47** and **s 20** the *mens rea* does not match the *actus reus*.

Actus reus

Assault or battery

Did D cause someone to apprehend immediate personal harm – **Ireland**? Was there an unlawful and direct application of force – **Thomas**? Assault or battery are common law offences but will be charged under **s 39 Criminal Justice Act 1988**.

It may be that a more serious offence under **OAPA 1861** has occurred. If so you could go straight to **s 47**, but remember you will then need to discuss assault or battery as one of these is needed for **s 47**.

Assault occasioning actual bodily harm

S 47 applies if harm has occurred following an assault (or battery). It includes most types of harm (**Miller**) but must be more than trivial (**Chan-Fook**). Ireland confirmed the word 'assault' in **s 47** is common assault so includes either assault or battery.

Then enlarge on any issues which are relevant to the given facts e.g. harm can now include psychiatric harm – **Ireland/Burstow 1997**, battery can be via another – **Haystead 1999**.

Discuss causation where this is an issue – was harm foreseeable? Did something happen that might break the chain of causation? (**Roberts/Cheshire**). Add the 'thin skull rule' if applicable (**Blaue**).

Unlawful and malicious wounding or inflicting/causing grievous bodily harm

Under **s 20** or **18** there must be a wound – **Eisenhower 1984** or serious harm **Smith/Saunders**.

Mens rea

Intent: can be direct (D's aim or purpose) or indirect (**Nedrick/Woollin** – was the result a virtual certainty, did D appreciate this). This usually only needs discussing for **s 18**

Subjective recklessness: D saw a risk of the result and went ahead anyway – **Cunningham**.

MR for **s 47** is intent or subjective recklessness as to the assault/battery not the resulting harm – **Roberts/Savage**.

MR for **s 20** is intent or subjective recklessness as to some harm, not serious harm – **Mowatt**.

MR for **s 18** is intent (only) to cause grievous bodily harm (**Parmenter**). If intent is not clear explain why and go onto **s 20** as an alternative.

Homicide – working through a problem

If the scenario shows someone has died, state and apply the homicide rules, briefly where obvious but in more detail where unclear. E.g., if X stabs Y with a huge knife there is no need for a long discussion of indirect intent (**Woollin**), nor usually of causation. However, causation may need discussing if Y was recovering and there was negligent hospital treatment, though this rarely breaks the chain of causation (**Cheshire**), it would need discussing.

Actus reus

Is there an unlawful killing of a human being by an act or omission?

If it was an omission was there a duty to act? – **Gibbins and Proctor/Pittwood/Khan**

Did the act or omission cause the death? – **White/Cheshire/Roberts**

Did AR and MR coincide? – **Fagan/Thabo Meli**

If you have established the *actus reus* of murder then go on to decide whether it is murder or manslaughter by applying the rules on *mens rea*.

Mens rea

Is there intent to kill or seriously injure? – **DPP v Smith 1961**

There may be direct intent (**Mohan**) or indirect intent. If direct intent is not clear, explain and apply the test from **Nedrick/Woollin**.

If mens rea is also established then it will be murder. However, there may be a defence to murder under the Homicide Act 1957 or the Coroners and Justice Act 2009.

Apply the rules on diminished responsibility and / or loss of control as appropriate.

Diminished responsibility – there must be an abnormality of mental functioning – apply **s 2** of the **1957 Act** as amended by the **2009 Act.**

Loss of control: there must be a qualifying trigger – apply **s 54 and 55** of the **2009 Act.**

If mens rea is not established then discuss involuntary manslaughter.

Apply the rules on unlawful and dangerous act manslaughter and / or gross negligence manslaughter as appropriate.

For unlawful and dangerous act manslaughter the act must be unlawful (**Lamb**), dangerous (**Church**) and have caused death (apply the rules on causation). The *mens rea* is that for the unlawful act (not the death).

For gross negligence manslaughter there must be a risk of death, a duty, breach of that duty and negligence so gross as to be deemed criminal (**Adomako** as confirmed in **Misra**).

Finally, you'll need to consider whether any of the general defences apply.

Examination tip

Before you start writing out your answer to an examination question read the question carefully and take a few minutes to do a quick plan, just with the main issues. This will act as a reminder to include all relevant points, especially if you run short of time. If this happens refer to your plan and deal with any remaining points at least briefly. If you leave something out altogether, you may prevent your answer getting into the top band, but if you have time to deal with the basics and the rest of the answer is sound, you can still get high marks.

The following examination questions are from AQA.

Read the questions carefully. Do a thorough plan for what you think you should cover. For questions 04 and 05, use the guides to working through a problem above and the application practice exercises in the relevant chapters. For 06, use the evaluation practice in chapters 1 and 2, and include a concluding paragraph in your plan.

January 2012: Scenario 2

When James repaired the brakes of the car owned by his neighbour, Harry, he was distracted by a conversation with his wife and forgot to tighten the bolts on one wheel. Shortly after Harry drove the car away, he saw his friend, Kim, walking towards him on the grass verge of the road. She was followed at a short distance by her friend, Lauren. As a joke, Harry decided to give Kim a bit of a scare by speeding up and driving at her. Kim realised that it was Harry and began to laugh. At that moment, the car wheel came off and the car veered off the road and into Kim, causing fatal injuries. Meanwhile, Lauren had hastily flung herself into a hedge, where her face and arms were ripped by thorns, leaving permanent scars.

Afterwards, Kim's father, Mike, began to suffer from anxiety and stress and became depressed and irritable. Unknown to him, Nora, his wife, began an affair with Oliver. One day in a bar, Mike overheard Oliver boasting to some friends about his physical abuse of women, and identifying Nora as his latest woman, "whose stupid daughter got herself run over and killed". Stunned, Mike brooded on this for about 45 minutes before he suddenly rushed over to Oliver, pushed him off the bar stool, and stamped three or four times on his head. Oliver had a previously undetected weakness of the skull and he suffered massive damage to his brain. Doctors treating him for his injuries decided that nothing more could be done. Oliver was pronounced dead after his life-support machine was switched off.

04 Discuss the possible criminal liability of Harry for the injuries to Lauren. Discuss the possible criminal liability of Harry and of James for the involuntary manslaughter of Kim. (25 marks + 5 marks for AO3)

05 Discuss the possible criminal liability of Mike for the murder of Oliver. (25 marks)

06 Despite some recent reforms, there are still criticisms to be made of the current law on murder and voluntary manslaughter. Consider relevant criticisms of that law, and suggest any reforms that may be appropriate. (25 marks)

January 2010: Scenario 1

I have given a middle-level answer for the following questions. Look at each of these and then expand where you think the answer is weak, or even wrong. There is a higher-grade answer for each question at the end of the book.

Encouraged by their friends whilst they were all being rowdy, Henry and Jack took part in a 'boxing match' in which each had one glove and both wore blindfolds. During the match, Henry had struck Jack twice in the face, leaving him with red marks and a small swelling under his eye. Jack then took out a knife which he had hidden in his pocket. Before anyone could intervene, Jack lashed out in Henry's direction but missed him and, instead, inflicted a deep cut on the arm of Karim, one of the friends who was watching. The cut required a large number of stitches.

Mike, Jack's father, had found it increasingly difficult to cope with the stress of modern life, including Jack's wild behaviour. Mike had developed a strong (but wholly unjustified) belief that he was being followed wherever he went, and that his life was in danger. Walking on the upper level of the shopping centre one day, he noticed Pete, who lived in the neighbourhood. Mike and Pete had recently had a number of arguments. Mike immediately assumed that Pete was "following" him, and shouted at him to go away. Pete shouted back, "If you keep on like that, someone will get you, you stupid old idiot." Pete then walked off but, a few minutes later, Mike suddenly ran at him and pushed him over the railing. Pete fell to the lower level, where he struck his head very heavily and died.

01 Consider the liability of Henry for the injuries to Jack, and the liability of Jack for the injuries to Karim. (25 marks)

Middle-level answer: Henry could be charged with ABH as he caused more than trivial harm (**Chan Fook**). ABH is an assault, which is an assault or battery, causing harm. There is a battery as he used force. Battery has no statutory definition but it is found in the **Criminal Justice Act** as a summary offence with a maximum of 6 months in prison. We can say that 'but for' his actions Jack would not have been harmed and also he made as significant contribution to Jack's injuries as required by **Cheshire**. As in Roberts nothing broke the chain of causation. He also had *mens rea* as he intended to cause him harm as it was a boxing match, it was at least virtually certain to cause harm and he must have realised this (**Nedrick**). Henry could argue that Jack consented to be harmed and this may succeed as it is a sporting situation as in AG's Reference.

Jack could be liable for **s 18** or **s 20** wounding which is an open cut Eisenhower. The first carries a maximum life sentence but the latter is only a maximum of 5 years. He used a knife so it could be **s 18** as this shows intent. Even if intent can't be proved he was reckless and this is enough for **s 20**. He could also use the defence of consent but it may not succeed in his case because the harm was serious.

02 Consider the liability of Mike for the murder of Pete. (25 marks)

Middle-level answer: The *actus reus* for murder is the killing of a human being as set out by Sir Edward Coke. Mike has caused a death as he made a significant contribution to it, as in **Cheshire**. The *mens rea* for murder is intent to kill or cause serious injury. If the jury believe he saw that his actions would certainly result in this then he has *mens rea* (**Nedrick**).

Loss of control is a partial defence to murder. This is found in the **Homicide Act 1957**. He must have lost control due to a qualifying trigger and this can be what was said to him. Whether another person of the same age and sex would have reacted the same way in the circumstances is looked at. The jury may decide that another person would have done the same in his circumstances, with his medical history. Under the new Act the loss of control need not be sudden so he may succeed in this defence.

Diminished responsibility is another partial defence to murder resulting in a conviction for manslaughter if successful. It is defined in the **Homicide Act 1957** as amended. The abnormality of mental functioning (**Byrne**) must result from a medical condition. This could be battered women's syndrome as in **Thornton** or something like depression etc. He is paranoid about people following him and this would be enough. Substantial impairment would be considered by reference to **Lloyd**.

03 In recent years, there has been much dissatisfaction with the current law of murder and voluntary manslaughter. Explain the reasons for this dissatisfaction and consider what proposals have been made for the reform of the law. (25 marks)

Middle-level answer: There are many problems in the law when someone has been intentionally killed. Murder is a common law offence. It is not clear whether someone who is 'brain dead' or a foetus in the womb is a human being. In **AGs Reference (No 3 of 1994)**, the HL held that a foetus was not a human being for the purpose of a murder conviction. However, if the foetus is injured and dies from that injury after being born, that could amount to murder.

The *mens rea* for murder is intent to kill or seriously injure, for such a serious crime it should be intent to kill. Also, the law on intent has developed but is arguably still unclear despite the **Nedrick** direction. There should be a statutory definition of murder.

What amounts to an 'abnormality' is difficult for the jury to understand and medical evidence is often complex and contradictory. The difficulties for the jury could lead to inconsistency. Diminished responsibility is sometimes dependent on whether the killing was morally wrong and juries may differ on this, also leading to inconsistency.

Diminished responsibility is not a satisfactory alternative for abused women who fail on loss of control as it indicates they are mentally unbalanced. Also, there is an overlap between diminished responsibility and loss of control where the killing has been due to a mental state such as depression or long-term abuse (**Aluwahlia** and **Thornton**) but the distinction isn't clear. The loss of control offence is easier to use for men who lash out on the spur of the moment, woman cannot usually do this as they will be subject to even more violence if they try. The law seems to apply equally but it doesn't in practice.

Answers 1 Murder

Exercise 1 Mellor 1996 and Corbett 1996

The failure to give him oxygen.

In **Cheshire 1991**.

Factual causation is shown by saying that 'but for' D's attack **Mellor** would not have been taken to hospital and would not have died from bronchial-pneumonia (**White**). Legal causation is shown by saying D's act was significant (**Cheshire**) and the poor hospital treatment was sufficiently foreseeable not to break the chain of causation (Roberts/Cheshire).

Roberts 1971, because she was also trying to escape but this was held to be a foreseeable reaction so did not break the chain of causation.

Exercise 2 Stringer 2008

That death or serious injury was a virtual certainty

It was a virtual certainty that somebody asleep upstairs would suffer at least serious harm from a fire being started at the bottom of the stairs. (In the actual case the CA held that the evidence that this was the case was overwhelming.)

That D appreciated that death or serious injury was a virtual certainty.

Even with a low IQ, the boy must have appreciated that somebody would suffer from a fire in the above circumstances. (The CA again held that the evidence for this was also overwhelming.)

Matthew & Alleyne (note the Q asked for a case *after* **Woollin**).

Exercise 3

Fagan	An act may be seen as continuing
Stone and Dobinson	Liability for an omission arises if there is a duty of responsibility for someone
Roberts	A foreseeable act will not break the chain of causation
Cheshire	D must make a significant contribution to the result
DPP v Smith	The *mens rea* of murder is satisfied by an intent to kill or seriously injure
Blaue	D must take V as found

Exercise 4 Application of the law to the case of Pagett:

This is a brief answer. In an examination, you will need to expand a little on the cases used in support to show why they are relevant.

Murder is the unlawful killing of a human being under the Queen's peace with malice aforethought (intent). The emphasis in **Pagett** is on both causation and *mens rea*.

Actus reus: Factual causation

Factual causation is established by using the 'but for' test (**White**). This test is satisfied because 'but for' Pagett holding the girl, she would not have died. He factually caused death.

Actus reus: Legal causation

To prove legal causation, it needs to be shown that Pagett made a significant contribution to the death (**Cheshire**) and also that nothing broke the chain of causation (**Cheshire, Roberts**). Pagett's action of holding her in front of him made a significant contribution to the girl's death. There is a possible intervening act, that of the police. However, the intervening act, of the police returning fire, was foreseeable and so did not break the chain of causation (**Roberts**). Pagett legally caused death.

Mens rea

The MR for murder is intent to kill or seriously injure (**Smith**). This means it was either D's aim to kill or seriously injure, (direct intent, **Mohan**) or death or serious injury was a virtual certainty and D appreciated this (oblique intent) (**Nedrick/Woollin**). It was not Pagett's aim to kill or seriously injure the girl so there is no direct intent.

Apply the rules on oblique intent. The jury will need to decide if Pagett himself (a subjective test) appreciated that death or serious injury was a 'virtual certainty'. This is debateable.

In conclusion, Pagett will probably be found not guilty of murder due to lack of *mens rea* but he will be guilty of manslaughter. This is in fact what he was found guilty of in the case itself.

Examination tip

It is acceptable to say 'probably' in your conclusions to exam questions as there is rarely a definite answer, especially if it is a decision for a jury, but do make an attempt to apply the law. In a scenario like this in an examination you would need to go on to explain and apply the law on manslaughter. There is an unlawful and dangerous act (shooting at the police) which causes death (refer back to above), you'll cover manslaughter later. You would also need to discuss any possible and relevant defences, which you also cover later.

Exercise 5 Evaluation practice

There is no 'right' answer to evaluation questions. You can form your own opinion but always use cases to back up what you say. What follows is a guide on what can be added to the comments, but you may have other, equally valid, ideas.

The law on intent lacks clarity

The current law is that intent can be found if, at the time of acting, D appreciated that death or serious injury was a virtually certain result of that action (**Nedrick/Woollin**). Use the cases on the development of the law on intent to show the different definitions used by judges and to discuss whether there is/has been a lack of clarity. Is the law more satisfactory since **Nedrick/Woollin**?

Comment: In **Woollin** Lord Hope said, "I attach great importance to the search for a direction which is both clear and simple .... I think that the **Nedrick** direction fulfils this requirement admirably"

Don't forget a criticism of the law should always recognise any positive changes.

The serious harm rule should be changed

Discuss whether it is right that someone can be convicted of murder where the intent is to cause serious harm rather than death, which is the current law – **DPP v Smith**.

The rule was confirmed in **Cunningham 1981** and although the Law Lords criticised it, they refused to overrule it, preferring to leave that to Parliament.

The Law Commission has also criticised it and in their 2006 report, Murder, Manslaughter and Infanticide, suggest splitting murder into first and second degree, as in the United States. If there was only intent to cause serious harm, it would usually be second-degree murder unless D knew there was a serious risk of death.

The Law Commission gives an example of D punching someone who falls and hits their head and dies of a brain haemorrhage. The act is wrong, but should it be murder? This is particularly controversial in light of the thin skull rule; splitting murder into first and second degree would seem fairer.

However, D must intend serious harm, so arguably this type of act should be murder, at least until the Commission's proposals are accepted (of which there is no sign).

Mercy killing should be made legal

Euthanasia, or 'mercy killing', is controversial. Under the current law, killing a loved one who is suffering and begs for relief from the pain will be murder, as the aim or purpose is to kill, so there will be direct intent. This intentional act has caused death, so both the *actus reus* and *mens rea* of murder are present. The same would apply to a doctor who took positive action to end someone's life. Although an omission to act has been held by the courts not to be murder – **Airedale NHS Trust v Bland**, this seems to be a decision based on morality rather than law. Arguably, withholding life-sustaining food and treatment is an act so strictly (and legally) speaking it should be murder. In **Gibbins & Proctor**, an omission to feed their daughter was held to be murder. **Bland** can be compared to **Cox 1992**, where a doctor gave an injection to a patient begging for help to die. This is a positive act, and the HL in Bland made clear that the ruling would not extend to such an act. Use any of the other mercy killing cases in support of an argument that the law should – or should not – make a distinction between a cold-blooded killing and a killing at the request of a terminally ill victim. You could also add that juries may make their decision on moral grounds rather than on the actual facts, because they are sympathetic to the difficulties D faced, so they may acquit when D clearly had an intention to kill. This means the judge cannot pass sentence at all. The cases of **Inglis** and **Gilderdale** highlight this problem.

Comment: Many of the cases seen with diminished responsibility involve mercy killing, so you can add other cases to this later when you have covered voluntary manslaughter

The mandatory sentence for murder should be abolished

There are valid arguments for and against the current law that all murder convictions result in a life sentence. Murder is very serious so a life sentence can be said to be appropriate, however there are different degrees of violence involved in murder cases and it seems wrong that all intentional killings attract the same sentence. The DPP and the Law Commission have both recommended that there should not be a mandatory life sentence; sentencing should be discretionary. This would allow judges to take the circumstances into account. Currently they can only make a recommendation of what 'life' should mean as a minimum or maximum. Refer to any of the euthanasia cases (**Inglis**, **Gilderdale**, **Cox** etc.) to support an argument that a fairer result may have been achieved if the judge had had discretion, or use other cases of your choice – as long as they are relevant. You could also mention that more people may be convicted if the mandatory sentence was abolished, because juries often don't want to convict where they know it means a life sentence so they may acquit even though they believe D is guilty of the murder, this means D is not sentenced at all.

Point out that the reforms suggested by the Law Commission on murder have not been accepted so the law of murder is still based on decisions by judges rather than Parliament.

Comment: As voluntary manslaughter only applies to murder cases, you could add a discussion of the two partial defences (see Answers 2) to an evaluation of murder.

Self-test questions

The actus reus *of murder is the unlawful killing of a human being under the queen's peace. The* mens rea *has been interpreted as malice aforethought, meaning an intent to kill or seriously injure.*

A result crime is one where a particular consequence is required as part of the actus reus. *Causation will therefore be important when proving* actus reus, *as D's actions must be the factual and legal cause of the result.*

The answer depends on which cases you chose; an example would be **Nedrick**. *The victim would not have died 'but for' his actions and it was foreseeable that someone could be seriously injured in an arson attack. (So he caused the death, but he was not guilty of murder because he did not have* mens rea.*)*

The 'virtual certainty' test for mens rea *was established in* **Nedrick 1986** *and confirmed by the HL in* **Woollin 1998**.

Exercise 6 Examination practice January 2012

This question requires a discussion of what the current law on murder is, and a critical examination of whether it is satisfactory. This can include issues in relation to the *actus reus* of murder, including liability for omissions and causation, and the *mens rea* issue in relation to malice aforethought and intent. The following key criticisms provide a base on which you can build for an essay. Choose ones that you feel you can explain well and expand on those; you are not expected to cover everything. Also refer to the previous exercise. The next section includes a critique of voluntary manslaughter which is also required for this question.

Key criticisms of actus reus, mens rea and murder

D is not usually liable for an omission but can be in certain circumstances, as in **Gibbins & Proctor**. This may appear harsh as it results in a life sentence for what many see as incompetence rather than malice. However, *mens rea* must also be proved so a person will only be guilty of murder where there is intent to kill or seriously injure.

There is a degree of uncertainty in some cases, e.g., **Bland** in relation to what amounts to an omission and **Fagan** and **Thabo Meli** in relation to coincidence of *actus reus* and *mens rea* and what amounts to a continuing act, or a series of acts.

Sometimes questions arise about whether someone who is 'brain dead' or a foetus in the womb is a human being. In **AGs Reference (No 3 of 1994) 1997**, the HL held that a foetus was not a human being for the purpose of a murder conviction. However, if the foetus is injured and dies from that injury after being born, that could amount to murder. Arguably, there should be greater clarity on this.

The rules on what will break the chain of causation may be difficult for a jury to understand.

The law on intent has developed but is arguably still unclear.

Murder is a common law offence. Should there be a statutory definition? If so, should it contain more than one degree of murder as in the USA? This could again remove the need for the special defences.

The *mens rea* for murder is intent to kill or seriously injure, for such a serious crime, should it only be intent to kill?

Exercise 7

It is possibly not true because she still needs to have lost control, even though it need not be sudden. The fact that she went to the kitchen to calm down before picking up the knife indicates she was in control of her actions.

The sexual infidelity issue was interpreted in **Clinton 2012** as meaning that it may be excluded if this was the only 'trigger' for the loss of control, but it could be included as part of the whole circumstances.

The statement refers to a *charge* of murder, rather than manslaughter. However, the charge would be murder in any case. It is the *conviction* that will be for manslaughter if the defence succeeds.

Although the threat to his son may qualify as a trigger for his loss of control, because **s 55** says the fear of violence from V may be 'against D or another identified person', Baillie might fail in the new defence because his actions could be seen as revenge. This is specifically excluded by **s 54(2)**. Much will depend on whether it is a 'considered desire' for revenge. He could also fail on the causation issue. Although there is no longer a need for the loss of control to be 'sudden and temporary', **s 54** requires that the killing 'resulted' from the loss of control. If he lost control and went immediately to the dealer's house he may succeed. However, if there was a significant time lapse between the loss of control at hearing of the threat and the killing he is unlikely to convince a jury that the killing was caused by the loss of control.

Doughty might fail because although he lost control because of 'things done or said' – the baby's crying – this is unlikely to be a qualifying trigger because **s 55** states that the 'things done or said' must be of an 'extremely grave character' and have caused D to have a 'justifiable sense of being seriously wronged'. A crying baby is not likely to be seen as either of these things, so it is probable that the defence would fail.

N.B.: It is possible the defence would have failed in these two cases before, both appeals succeeded because the matter was never allowed to go before a jury.

Exercise 8 Case study on Clinton 2012

S 55(6)

Fear of serious violence and / or things said or done which constitute constituted circumstances of an extremely grave character, and caused D to have a justifiable sense of being seriously wronged.

The judge thought the wife's infidelity should be ignored because it is excluded by **s 55(6)**.

The CA disagreed.

Sexual infidelity has an effect as the CA said it should be treated as an integral part of the overall circumstances.

A retrial was ordered because the jury should have been able to consider the defence of loss of control (based on the fact that the infidelity was part of the whole).

The defence of loss of control is not allowed if D acted in a 'considered desire for revenge'	S 54(4) Coroners and Justice Act 2009
The loss of self-control does not need to be sudden	S 54(2) Coroners and Justice Act 2009
Sexual infidelity may be relevant to the circumstances of D, even though excluded by s 55	Clinton 2012
An 'abnormality of mind' (now mental functioning) for diminished responsibility is one that reasonable people would term abnormal	Byrne 1960
The abnormality of mental functioning must provide an explanation for D's acts and omissions in doing or being a party to the killing	S 2(1)(c) Homicide Act as amended
An abnormality caused by alcoholism may be accepted as diminished responsibility	Tandy 1989
Impairment of responsibility need not be total but must be more than trivial	Lloyd 1967
Where there is evidence of intoxication as well as another cause of 'abnormality' the jury should ignore the intoxication	Dietschmann 2003

Exercise 10 Case study on Freaney

Mrs Freaney was charged with murder and pleaded diminished responsibility

If successful, the defence reduces the charge to manslaughter and this is important because it gives the judge discretion in sentencing

That D was suffering from an abnormality of mental functioning which:

(a) arose from a recognised medical condition,

(b) substantially impaired D's ability to do one or more of the things mentioned in

subsection (1A),

(c) provides an explanation for D's act or omission

She would first need to show that she was suffering from an 'abnormality of mental functioning' at the time of the killing. Under the old law, in **Byrne 1960**, it was said that 'abnormality of mind' meant a state of mind so different from that of normal human beings that the reasonable man would deem it abnormal. It is likely that abnormality of mental functioning will be interpreted in the same way. The abnormality must arise from a 'recognised medical condition'. Severe stress is likely to amount to a recognised medical condition. In **Gittens 1984**, chronic depression was accepted as such, so the 'abnormality' arose from, or was caused by, the severe stress. She will then need to convince the jury that the abnormality of mental functioning, which arose from her stress, substantially impaired her ability to do one of the 3 things set out in **s 52**. These are a) to understand the nature of her conduct; (b) to form a rational judgement; (c) to exercise self-control. In **Lloyd 1967**, the court held that substantial did not mean total but the impairment must be more than trivial. She seemed to understand the nature of her conduct, but it is possible she could not form a rational judgement due to the stress. It is also arguable that she was unable to exercise self-control at the time of the killing. The abnormality of mental functioning would appear to have caused, or at least significantly have contributed to, the killing of her son. Her plea of diminished responsibility is likely to succeed under the new law, so she would be convicted of manslaughter, not murder.

Exercise 11 Application practice

Wood could plead the defence of diminished responsibility under the **Homicide Act** as amended. Alcohol dependency syndrome would be a recognised medical condition, so we must consider whether the abnormality arose from this. In the case itself the CA thought it could have and quashed the conviction, and this is likely still to be the case. According to **Dietschmann**, D need not show that he would have killed even if sober; the intoxication can be ignored by the jury as long as there is also an abnormality of mental functioning. If the abnormality arose from a recognised condition (the alcohol dependency syndrome) then Wood would probably succeed in the defence as it seems to have substantially impaired his ability to control himself. If he argued the defence of loss of control under the **Coroners and Justice Act** this is more likely to fail. He appears to have lost control as the attack was 'frenzied', but the loss of control must be triggered by something set out in **s 55(1)** of the Act. He was not in fear of violence, but he has reacted to 'things done'. The issue will be whether these constituted 'circumstances of an extremely grave character', and caused him to have a 'justifiable sense of being seriously wronged'. It could go either way.

Exercise 12 Evaluation practice

The removal of the need for a 'sudden and temporary' loss of control is an improvement. However, the fact that any loss of control must be shown goes against the Law Commission's proposals and prevents the defence clearly extending to cases of abuse against women, who may be physically weaker and liable to even greater abuse if they lose control and fight back. Also the fact that acting in a desire for revenge is excluded arguably brings back an element of the 'sudden and temporary' requirement.

The inclusion of a fear of serious violence as a qualifying trigger may help in cases where someone is reacting to violence but does not meet the requirements for the defence of self-defence. It could solve some of the problems with the 'all or nothing' nature of self-defence where juries may be reluctant to accept it feeling that D should not be totally acquitted. In a murder case, the loss of control defence may be a more suitable alternative as D is not acquitted but sentenced at the judge's discretion.

Reference to a recognised medical condition is clearer than the old law on diminished responsibility, which was complex and hard for juries to understand. However, a problem that remains is one that the Law Commission recognised. They had recommended that developmental immaturity in those under 18 should be included within the definition of diminished responsibility as a recognised medical condition. This was because there is evidence to show that parts of the brain which play an important role in the development of self-control do not mature until 14 years of age. The Government did not act on this suggestion. To an extent, it is covered where the lack of maturity is caused by a medical disorder such as autism, but this clearly will not cover all young defendants so a child of 10 or over who kills can be convicted of murder even where there is evidence they had an abnormality of mental functioning due to their immaturity.

The 'qualifying triggers' are fear of serious violence or thing(s) done and/or said which not only constituted circumstances of an extremely grave character but also caused D to have a justifiable sense of being seriously – or a combination of these

The Act excludes sexual infidelity as a qualifying trigger

S 54(3) *excludes characteristics, or circumstances, whose only relevance to D's conduct is that they bear on D's general capacity for tolerance or self-restraint. Examples include a short-temper or drunkenness*

Medical evidence will be required for a defence of diminished responsibility

The accused has the burden of proving the defence

Sexual infidelity is excluded as a qualifying trigger

Dietschmann 2003

Dowds 2012

When it results from a recognised illness, stated in **Tandy 1989**

Exercise 13 Examination practice January 2012

Refer back to the answer guide for the murder question in the last chapter; you need to cover both areas. This guide only covers a critique of voluntary manslaughter. Remember, you are not expected to cover everything so choose ones that you feel you can explain well and expand on those. Refer also to the answer guide for exercise 12. Here are a few pointers.

Diminished responsibility is not a satisfactory alternative for abused women as it indicates they are mentally unbalanced.

Where there is evidence of intoxication as well as another cause of 'abnormality' the jury has to perform an almost impossible task of separating the one from the other – **Dietschmann**.

'Abnormality of mental functioning' is difficult for the jury to understand and medical evidence is often complex and contradictory.

Diminished responsibility is sometimes dependent on whether the killing was morally wrong – **Bailey/Sutcliffe.**

Success may depend on which defence is raised in the first place. What was then provocation failed in the case of **Cocker 1989**, but diminished responsibility succeeded in **Bailey 2002** in similar circumstances.

There is an overlap between diminished responsibility and loss of control where the killing has been due to a mental state such as depression or long-term abuse (**Aluwahlia** and **Thornton**).

Loss of control is still required, against the LC's recommendations, so the above two cases may well still fail even though it was cases like them that prompted calls for changes to the old law.

The difficulties of these defences for the jury could lead to inconsistency. Juries may differ in their decisions.

You are specifically asked about reforms so note where reforms have been made but add where you think the new law has not fully addressed previous criticisms. Exercise 12 should help with this, but also the above points could be expanded a little. You could include the fact that the revenge issue effectively brings the sudden and temporary rule back; that sexual infidelity should not have been excluded as a trigger – and is anyway a difficult term to be clear about – but that judges may assist in addressing this when interpreting the new law, as in **Clinton**. It can be said that the new law has brought in some clarification but is much stricter than the LC envisaged. This applies to the triggers for loss of control, which may exclude many situations which could have allowed the previous defence of provocation (e.g., **Doughty**) and to the narrower scope of the diminished responsibility rules which may exclude people to whom the new law was intended to apply (e.g., **Thornton**). Conclude as to what you think further reforms should be, e.g., take out the loss of control requirement, allow sexual infidelity as a trigger, include developmental immaturity. Reform of the mandatory sentence for murder and / or the introduction of a three-tiered structure for homicide (as the Law Commission recommended) would also meet many of the criticisms raised here and could mean the special defences were not needed at all.

For more information on the problems and reforms of murder and voluntary manslaughter go to the Law Commission website. Look in the A-Z at the 2004 report on 'Partial defences to murder' or the 2006 report on Murder, manslaughter and infanticide'. Quotes and discussions from these will enhance an essay and help you see how far the Coroners and Justice Act took up the LC's suggestions.

Answers 3 Involuntary manslaughter

Exercise 14 Case study on Evans

The most likely charge is gross negligence manslaughter. Unlawful act manslaughter would be less likely to succeed because V self-injected so there was no unlawful act which caused death (**Kennedy**). In addition, D appealed on the basis that she owed no duty so this indicates that a duty is required; this only applies to gross negligence manslaughter.

Stone and Dobinson or **Gibbins & Proctor** could support this charge as both involved a duty of care to a relative.

Adomako is the leading case.

The main elements of this charge are that there is a duty of care, that duty had been breached; the breach of duty amounted to gross negligence, and the negligence was a substantial cause of death. The test was restated in **Misra 2004.**

The test from **Adomako** needs to be applied. In respect of the mother there is a duty of care due to relationship as in **Gibbins and Proctor**. The duty is not so clear for D as she is only a half-sister, not a parent. **Stone and Dobinson** could support an argument for a duty based on a voluntary assumption of responsibility for another person. The facts here are similar because nothing was done to get medical help. Also, the facts can be related to **Miller**, where he had created a dangerous situation and did nothing to eliminate the risk. He was held to have owed a duty to act. This can be applied here because D bought the heroin and gave it to V, so can be said to have created a risky situation. In addition, the victim had showed symptoms of overdosing but was merely put to bed with no medical help. D did nothing to eliminate the risk, e.g., by getting medical help so breached her duty.

The Court of Appeal made clear in **Misra** that there must also be a risk of death. Here there is a risk of death because she had overdosed and neither D nor her mother attempted to get medical help. On the facts given, the duty appears to have been breached because D's actions did not reach the standard of the reasonable person; a reasonable person would get medical help. The final step is to decide if D's actions were sufficiently bad to be seen as 'grossly negligent', i.e., her conduct was so bad in all the circumstances as to amount to a criminal act or omission. This is a matter for the jury so could be argued either way. In conclusion, if the jury agree her conduct was sufficiently bad to be deemed criminal, D is guilty of manslaughter, and this appears to be the case as she was convicted. Her appeal is unlikely to succeed because, as discussed above, there appears to be supporting case law for the finding of a duty, and this was the element she appealed on.

The appeal failed. The CA found a duty to exist because D had created a state of affairs which she knew (or should have known) had become life threatening. If a person created, or contributed to, a situation which was life threatening then a duty to take reasonable steps to save that life would arise.

Exercise 15 case study on Willoughby

Gross negligence manslaughter.

Unlawful act manslaughter was seen as more appropriate. This is probably because it would be easier to prove, and the law is much clearer. Instead of applying the test from **Adomako**, all that would be needed would be to find an unlawful act which was dangerous and caused death.

For unlawful act manslaughter it first needs to be shown that there is an unlawful act. It must be criminally unlawful (**Lamb**). Setting fire to a building is arson and this is a crime. Next, it needs to be shown that it was dangerous. This is an objective test (**Church**) so it is whether a reasonable person would see it as dangerous, it does not matter whether Willoughby saw it that way. I believe that a jury would (as reasonable people) see that setting fire to something is dangerous, particular when petrol is used as an accelerant. The act caused death because the fire caused an explosion which caused the building to collapse, so there is no intervening act to break the chain of causation. An explosion following a fire is foreseeable (**Roberts/Pagett**). The act of setting the fire also made a significant contribution to the death of the taxi driver (**Cheshire**). The only thing remaining to be shown is that Willoughby also had *mens rea*. There is no special *mens rea* for this type of manslaughter; it is the *mens rea* for whatever the unlawful act is. This is likely to be subjective recklessness (**Cunningham**). If Willoughby saw the risk of fire and went ahead anyway this will be enough. It does not need to be shown he saw the risk of death, or even harm, only that he saw the risk of the unlawful act (arson) occurring. On the facts, it appears that the fire was intentional so there would be no problem finding *mens rea*.

Examination tip

You may not always know what the crime in a scenario is; here it is arson which is a type of criminal damage. If you haven't studied this just treat it as I did above, the vast majority of crimes require this type of *mens rea* (two exceptions being murder and theft which require intent).

Exercise 16

In **Hancock and Shankland**, the most appropriate type of manslaughter would be unlawful act manslaughter. This is because throwing the stone is criminal damage which is unlawful and it is clearly a dangerous act as viewed by reasonable people (**Church**). The driver would not have died 'but for' the Ds throwing the stone and throwing the stone made a significant contribution to the death. There is nothing to indicate the chain of causation would be broken so the Ds caused the death of the driver by their unlawful actions.

In **Stone & Dobinson**, the most appropriate type of manslaughter would be gross negligence manslaughter. This is because they owed his sister a duty of care by taking on responsibility for her. In not getting treatment, they breached this duty and as she was ill, there was a risk of death (**Adomako/Misra**). Their negligence caused the death because 'but for' their lack of care she would probably not have died, and this omission made a significant contribution to her death.

In **Nedrick**, the most appropriate type of manslaughter would be unlawful act manslaughter. This is because setting the fire is arson, a type of criminal damage, and so an unlawful act. Setting a fire is likely to be seen as dangerous by reasonable people (**Church**). Also 'but for' the fire the victim would not have died and the setting of the fire made a significant contribution to the death.

Exercise 17 application practice

In the first case, it could be unlawful act manslaughter. Your action may be unlawful (an assault), but would it be seen as dangerous? If not, and much may depend on whether she is obviously of a nervous disposition, you are not guilty of Cathy's manslaughter. If **Dawson** is followed you will not be guilty, if **Watson** is felt more appropriate then you could be guilty. If your action is seen as dangerous following **Watson**, then the fact that Cathy had a nervous disposition will not make a difference. Under the 'thin-skull' rule you must take her as you find her so will be liable for the full consequences (**Blaue**).

In the second, your action is unlawful because there is an assault (she apprehends violence from you) and any kind of assault is potentially dangerous, though this is a matter for the jury. The next question is whether you caused Kate's death. You cannot argue that most people would not have died, and that Kate's nervous disposition caused her death. As above, you must take your victim as you find her – **Blaue**. If the jury regard the act as dangerous then you are likely to be found guilty of manslaughter.

In the third, it may be gross negligence manslaughter. However although you owe the girl in your care a duty and have breached this by leaving her alone, it is unlikely that there was a risk of death as required by **Misra**. It is also unlikely that your action would be deemed sufficiently negligent to be criminal, though this is a matter for the jury and so arguable either way. Finally, it is unlikely to be found that your leaving her caused her death; you will argue that the driver who ran her over broke the chain of causation. As it is not foreseeable that she would be run over, you will probably succeed.

As the fire was accidental, there is no unlawful act. Here again it may be gross negligence manslaughter. You would not usually owe a duty to the caretaker but based on **Miller** it can be argued that you had a duty to act by creating a dangerous situation. The case of **Evans** supports this because the CA held that if a person created, or contributed to, a situation which was life threatening then a duty to take reasonable steps to save that life would arise. Fire is likely to be seen to create a risk of death (**Misra**) and you have breached your duty by not taking reasonable steps to either put out the fire or tell someone about it. However, it is possible that your action would not be deemed sufficiently negligent to be criminal, though as above, this is a matter for the jury and so arguable either way.

Self-test questions

A risk of death, a duty of care, breach of that duty and gross negligence as regards that breach, which must be sufficient to justify criminal liability

*It is possible to commit gross negligence manslaughter by omission if there is a duty to act, but not unlawful act manslaughter – **Khan***

D knocked a woman unconscious and then, wrongly believing her to be dead, threw her in the river to dispose of the 'body'. The principle was that if reasonable people would see the risk of harm, this will be enough to show it was 'dangerous'

*In **Cato**, D was guilty of manslaughter because he helped to administer the drug. In **Dalby** the chain of causation was broken by the victim's own act*

In the case of a fully informed adult self-administering the drug it would never be appropriate to find the supplier guilty of manslaughter

Exercise 18

Assault occasioning actual bodily harm.

Common assault, specifically battery. This is because he held her down and cut her hair, and even touching her clothes would have been enough according to **Thomas.**

The main reason was that hair was part of the body and was attached to it.

Miller 1954

Chan-Fook 1994

Applying the law on ABH, it can be seen that there is clearly a battery. Even touching someone's clothes can amount to battery (**Thomas**), and here he has held her down and cut her hair. He also intended to do this as he used scissors; he therefore has both *actus reus* and *mens rea* for battery. To establish ABH the only extra requirement is that his actions caused harm; there is no need to show *mens rea* for such harm. There is no issue with causation itself but there is an issue as to whether cutting hair amounts to bodily harm. In **Miller**, it was said that anything that interferes with health or comfort would suffice, and she arguably suffered discomfort. However, in **Chan-Fook** it was said that trivial harm should be excluded, so following this we could argue it is not enough for bodily harm. Using these cases, you can conclude he should be guilty of battery and that if, as Judge P said, hair is found to be part of the body then the battery has caused harm so he should be guilty of ABH.

Exercise 19 Case study on GBH

Horsley could certainly be found guilty of assault occasioning actual bodily harm even if he had not pleaded guilty, as he verbally assaulted her outside the restaurant and committed a battery by pouring bleach on her. He did both these with direct intent so *mens rea* is proved. The act caused her hair to turn white and she was mentally scarred by the incident so harm was more than trivial (**Chan-Fook**) and there is no causation issue. Also, no further *mens rea* is needed so we have ABH. It could be that the prosecution would succeed in the more serious charge of grievous bodily harm under either **s 20** or **s 18**. In both cases the *actus reus* is to inflict (or cause) serious harm (**Saunders**). Although prompt attention prevented her from suffering serious burns her mental scarring may suffice, as it was confirmed in the joint appeals of Ireland and **Burstow** that psychiatric harm could amount to GBH. It is likely that the jury would convict him of GBH. The question then is under which section? **S 20** would be reasonably easy to establish as he must have foreseen the risk (**Cunningham**) of some harm (**Mowatt**). It may well be that the jury will believe that even if serious harm wasn't his aim or purpose (**Mohan**) he must have appreciated that it was a virtual certainty (**Nedrick/Woollin**) as bleach can cause serious burns. They may therefore decide that he had indirect intent to cause serious harm and so deliver a verdict of guilty under **s 18**.

(In the case, he was convicted of **s 18** GBH)

Exercise 20 Case principles

An assault can be negated by words	**Turbeville v Savage 1669** His words indicated that he would not take any action, so there was no assault

Words can be enough for an assault (two 1997 cases)	**Constanza 1997** Stalking could come under assault, silence is enough, but the court also said words alone could amount to an assault **Ireland 1997** Telephone calls could amount to an assault, even silent ones
Silence can be enough for an assault (1983 and/or 1997 case)	**Smith v Chief Superintendent of Woking Police Station 1983** Silence can be an assault, e.g., a peeping Tom **Constanza 1997** Stalking could come under assault, i.e., silence is enough to amount to assault (or you can use **Ireland**)
A battery can be indirect (1990 case)	**DPP v K** Putting acid in a drier could amount to a battery on the person using it, even though there was no direct act
Mere emotions such as fear, distress or panic are not enough for actual bodily harm	**Chan Fook 1994** Mental, or psychiatric, harm could amount to actual bodily harm, but it must be some kind of medical condition
A foreseeable action by the victim will not break the chain of causation	**Roberts 1971** If the victim does something foreseeable in response to D's actions, D will still be said to have caused any harm that results
D does not need *mens rea* for the harm, only the assault	**Savage & Parmenter 1992** Throwing beer intentionally would be battery, if harm results then this makes it a s47 offence without any further *mens rea*
Grievous means serious harm	**Saunders 1985** Any serious harm will amount to GBH, it need not be 'really serious'
Wound means an open cut	**Eisenhower 1983** An internal injury could amount to grievous bodily harm, but not wounding, the skin must be broken
The HL confirmed that psychiatric harm can come under **s47, 18** or **20** (a 1997 joint appeal)	**Ireland & Burstow 1997** Which offence is appropriate will depend on whether the psychiatric harm is 'serious' (s20), serious and intended (s 18) or not serious (s47)

Exercise 21 Application practice

Goran pulled at Lisa's jacket and she fell over, grazing her knee

Battery is the most appropriate offence. Even touching clothes can amount to battery, **Thomas**. A graze does not seem enough for **s 47** assault occasioning actual bodily harm, but it is a possible alternative; there is a battery which has caused harm (a graze) and in **DPP v Smith** even cutting someone's hair was said to amount to bodily harm. Finally, even though the skin is broken (**Eisenhower**) it is not likely to be seen as serious enough to amount to wounding under **s 20**.

Tracey threw a book at Sam who jumped aside and pushed over an elderly woman, who cried out in pain

It may be assault if Sam was in fear of immediate personal violence. It would be a question of whether he saw it coming and, as he 'jumped aside', it appears he did. If the book hit him it would be battery. It is an indirect battery (**Haystead**) on the elderly woman which appears to have resulted in harm as she 'cried out in pain'. If the harm is more than trivial (**Chan-Fook**), Tracey can be liable under **s 47**. She need not intend any harm; it is enough that she intended the battery (**Savage**). An alternative approach would be to use the principle of transferred malice (**Latimer**); she had the *mens rea* for an assault on Sam and this can be transferred to the woman.

The woman had brittle bones and broke her leg when she fell

The thin skull rule applies (**Blaue**) so Tracey can be liable for the full results of her original action. Broken bones will be serious harm (**Saunders**) so it appears that it could be GBH **s 20**, however for that she needs to have intended, or at least been reckless as to 'some harm' (**Mowatt**) and this may be hard to prove. It is probably more appropriate to charge her under **s 47**; she has *mens rea* for a battery on Sam and the *actus reus* of causing harm to the elderly woman. The act of Sam jumping out of the way is foreseeable so it does not break the chain of causation (**Roberts**).

Tom sent a text message to Ahmed saying he will beat him next time he sees him

This would be assault, assuming that Ahmed is frightened by the threat, words or even silence can amount to assault (**Smith v Chief Superintendent of Woking Police Station 1983**). The question is whether the fear is of immediate harm. It is clear from **Ireland** that a telephone call will suffice and that 'immediate' is interpreted widely but you may need more information, e.g., if they lived a long way apart then Ahmed will not be in fear of immediate harm, but if they live nearby then an assault charge is more likely to succeed.

Pete lashed out at Ben with a knife, cutting his cheek

The skin is broken (**Eisenhower**) so this amounts to wounding under **s 18** or **20**. The use of a weapon (the knife) suggests that serious harm was intended so this is likely to be **s 18** wounding with intent.

Exercise 22 Evaluation practice

You would not be expected to cover all the problems in the law, but you could select 3 or 4 from the list below and expand on them and the relevant cases, or discuss more but in less detail. Choose ones that you feel you can explain well and expand on those. Proposals for reform mostly come from the original Law Commission proposals from Report 218 as the new Law Commission project will not be complete until the autumn of 2013. I have mentioned the latter where there is already an idea of reforms or because the proposals are likely to be as they were.

The negative point:

Assault and battery are still not included in statute law but left to judicial reasoning alone

The positive point and / or proposal for reform:

*The law can be developed to meet new situations and adapt to technological and social changes. For example, mobile phone technology means a telephone call is more likely to cause fear of immediate harm (**Ireland**) and so amount to an assault*

The negative point:

The word assault is ambiguous; it means the specific offence of causing someone to apprehend immediate personal violence (**Ireland**) but also means both an assault and a battery for the purpose of finding an 'assault' which occasions harm for **s 47**

> *The positive point and / or proposal for reform:*
>
> *The Law Commission (Report no. 218) proposed replacing assault and battery with a single new offence of assault but which would include the definitions of assault and battery*

The negative point:

The vocabulary in the **1861 Act** is outdated and unclear. Words such as 'whosoever', 'occasioning', 'grievous' and 'maliciously' are not in common use today and may anyway have meant something different in 1861 when the Act was written

> *The positive point and / or proposal for reform:*
>
> *The 2012/13 project by the Law Commission (LC) will look at modernising and simplifying the language*

The negative point:

The structure of the offences is illogical, as are the section numbers. This is partly because the Act was a consolidated one drawing from several sources but it means that the distinction between the offences is unclear

> *The positive point and / or proposal for reform:*
>
> *The 2012/13 project by the LC will look at restructuring the offences, perhaps into a kind of hierarchy. This would clarify not only the different levels of harm (actus reus) and fault (mens rea) but also sentencing*

The negative point:

It seems harsh that no *mens rea* is required for **s 47** for the harm caused, only for the assault or battery (**Savage**)

> *The positive point and / or proposal for reform:*
>
> *This is arguably implied in the Act which says an assault occasioning ABH, so once you have an assault all you need to make it a s 47 offence is that harm results.*
> *The LC proposed replacing s 47 ABH with an offence of intentional or reckless injury and requiring mens rea for the injury caused and this is likely to be repeated in the new project*

The negative point:

The meaning of 'immediate' in assault (and ABH) is vague

> *The positive point and / or proposal for reform:*
>
> *The courts have interpreted 'immediate' widely so that a phone call or stalking can be enough to put V in fear of 'immediate' harm (**Ireland / Constanza / Smith**) which means the law is keeping up with new technology*

The negative point:

S 47 and **s 20**: the sentencing maximums seem illogical as both sections carry the same maximum but they are very different offences

> *The positive point and / or proposal for reform:*

The judge can take into account the level of harm as well as the level of intent when sentencing (although cannot go beyond the maximum).
The LC will look at this is their 2012/13 project

The different wording of **s 18** and **s 20**, with 'causing' in the former and 'inflicting' in the latter, is misleading

The positive point and / or proposal for reform:

*The uncertainty between 'cause' and 'inflict' has been clarified by the HL in **Ireland & Burstow** where both **Salisbury** and **Wilson** were approved.*
The LC will, however, look at this is their 2012/13 project

S 18 and **20**: Essentially these two sections contain 4 different offences, reckless GBH, reckless wounding, GBH with intent and wounding with intent, which is confusing

The positive point and / or proposal for reform:

The LC proposed 2 offences, intentionally causing serious injury and recklessly causing serious injury and will look at this in their 2012/13 project

S 18 and **20**: A wound can be any cut (**Eisenhower**) which means that technically a small cut could amount to a wound but these are serious offences

The positive point and / or proposal for reform:

*The LC proposals are for the offence to be 'causing serious injury' with intent or recklessness, so a small cut will not be enough. Judges have also developed the law so that the age of the victim is a relevant factor in deciding on whether the harm is serious enough for GBH (**Bollom**) which seems sensible*

S 20: It seems harsh that no *mens rea* is required for serious harm, only for **some** harm (**Mowatt**)

The positive point and / or proposal for reform:

*The LC proposed replacing **s 20** with 'reckless serious injury' and requiring mens rea for the serious injury caused. Wounding would not be a separate offence but come under **s 18** or **20** depending on whether the wound was serious or not and whether it was intended*

S 18: It seems harsh that the *mens rea* as regards the harm caused is only recklessness, not intent, when resisting arrest **(Morrison)**

The positive point and / or proposal for reform:

*The LC proposed replacing **s 18** with 'intentional serious injury' and removing the part on resisting arrest. Wounding would be as above. These offences will both be looked at in the new project*

Self-test questions

Causation is important because ABH is a result crime. The assault or battery must have caused the resulting harm

Something no reasonable person could foresee could break the chain of causation

*Wound was interpreted as an open cut in **Eisenhower***

*GBH was interpreted as serious harm in **Saunders** (really serious harm in the earlier case of **Smith** is acceptable)*

*The mens rea for **s 20** is intent or recklessness to inflict some harm, but for **s 18** there must be intent (only) to cause serious harm*

Exercise 23 Examination practice

AQA June 2011

The non-fatal offences against the person have been subjected to frequent criticism. Explain and discuss these criticisms, and suggest what reforms might be desirable. (25 marks)

Look at the previous exercise for plenty of things to discuss. You should pick those that you feel you can explain most clearly and expand a little on them; there are so many criticisms and proposals for reform that you cannot cover them all.

One other point you could mention is the defence of consent (covered in **Chapter 5**). Consent can be used for certain levels of harm but not others and the law remains unclear on this (e.g., **Brown** compared to **Wilson**). Consent is implied in sports but not for all incidents. Refer to the next section for more.

Exercise 24

The Law Commission says the question is "When should a person not be criminally liable because of their mental condition at the time they committed an alleged offence?"

D's mental condition at the time the offence was committed is what is relevant.

'Sane automatism' is when D lacked conscious control of his/her actions at the time of committing the alleged offence for a reason other than his/her mental condition.

The rules on insanity come from **M'Naghten's case 1843.**

The Law Commission say is not clear whether the defence of insanity is even available in all cases.

The Law Commission says the defence is "underused".

This is because the law lags behind psychiatric understanding.

The problem regarding evidence from medical professionals is that they do not apply the correct legal test.

The Law Commission says that the term 'insane' is outdated as a description of those with mental illness.

The Law Commission says that the term 'insane' is simply wrong as regards those who have learning disabilities, learning difficulties or epilepsy.

A case example of when epilepsy was classed as insanity is **Sullivan 1984.**

The Law Commission says that the problem with the case law on these two defences is that it is incoherent and produces results that run counter to common sense.

The other potential problem highlighted is that the defences may not comply with the **European Convention on Human Rights.**

Exercise 25 Case study on Marison

The act must be involuntary, so there must be a total loss of control which is not self-induced. Here he could not rely on automatism because he knew that such an incident could occur. It had happened before.

Broome v Perkins 1987 or **Attorney-General's Reference (No2 of 1992)**. The defence failed in both as D had retained some control over his driving.

It was held that getting intoxicated was reckless in **Majewski.**

Where the offence is one of specific intent. This was stated in **Bailey.**

The point was that automatism could succeed because he took the drugs thinking they would calm him down, so the effect they had was unexpected and did not amount to being 'self-induced'. A distinction was made between these sorts of drugs and those known to be unpredictable where the defence would fail (e.g., LSD).

He was not reckless because the drugs were supposed to calm him and he could not foresee the actual effects.

The defence of insanity could have succeeded because diabetes is an internal factor and so a disease of the mind, but he would have to show that he did not know what he was doing.

Because he did not know the drugs would have unpredictable results, he thought they would calm him.

No. In such cases, the defence can succeed for both basic and specific intent crimes, as D has not been reckless.

Intoxication will be an external factor, not an internal one, so the insanity defence would fail if the disease of the mind is cause by drink or drugs. As regards automatism, this defence could succeed, but it will depend on the intoxicant. If D took a sedative, particularly one which was prescribed, the defence could succeed, but if the drug is unpredictable (alcohol will always be seen as unpredictable, as will most recreational drugs) the defence will fail as any loss of control will be seen as self-induced.

Exercise 26 Consent principles

Consent is never a defence to murder **- Pretty**

Consent must be true consent, so a child may not be deemed to have consented - **Burrell & Harmer**

Consent can make even serious violence in sports lawful - **Barnes**

There must be consent to harm, not just to sex - **Dica**

The CA set out some examples of when consent could be implied - **A-G's Reference (No 6 of 1980)**

Consent may be a valid defence even for serious harm if it is seen as 'rough horseplay' - **Aitken**

Exercise 27 Self-defence

She was charged with grievous bodily harm with intent and an alternative charge of inflicting grievous bodily harm.

These offences arise under **s 18 and 20 of the Offences against the Person Act 1861.**

She pleaded self-defence and the judge ruled there was no evidence to counter her argument that she kicked out in self-defence.

The requirements for this defence are that D honestly believed the action was justified and only reasonable force was used.

According to **McInnes**, D need not retreat.

Applying the law to the facts, she genuinely believed that he was attempting to attack her and that her action was justified. He had been "violent towards her in the past", and had slapped her earlier the same evening, which would make her belief he was going to attack her appear genuine. As long as it is genuine, her belief can be mistaken (**Williams**).

In these particular circumstances, it is unclear whether the force was reasonable. She could not retreat as she was in the back of a moving car so there is no issue with that point. She caused serious injury but she had only 'kicked out' from the back of the car so this may be seen as reasonable force, even though the consequences were that she caught him in the eye with her stiletto heel. The judge seemed to believe this was reasonable force as he said to the jury "There is no evidence to lead you to the conclusion the defendant was not acting in instinctive, reasonable self-defence."

One problem that arises is that she succeeded even though she was "heavily intoxicated with drink". In **O'Grady** and **Hatton,** it was made clear that the defence should not succeed if D is intoxicated when mistakenly believing the action to be justified, and this is repeated in **s 76** of the **Criminal Justice and Immigration Act 2008**. This means a mistaken belief (e.g., that he was going to attack her) need not be reasonable but is not usually allowed if it is a drunken mistake.

Firstly, note that you were told that the charge was manslaughter (perhaps because the prosecution thought it might be hard to prove *mens rea*). This means that, even though some of the phrases could suggest diminished responsibility or loss of control, these only apply to murder so will not be relevant for this question.

Hari was unreasonably convinced that everyone was plotting against him, and he ...

*This indicates that insanity should be discussed as the word 'unreasonably' indicates Hari was not thinking rationally (has a defect of reason) and is paranoid, (a disease of the mind). The defence could succeed, depending on whether Hari knew what he was doing was wrong when he killed (**Windle 1952**). If he did he will be guilty of manslaughter, if not there will be a special verdict of guilty by reason of insanity and he will be subject to one of four orders.*

Irena was a diabetic who had taken her insulin, but had not eaten regularly and during a fit she ...

*If there is a defect of reason it was not caused by the diabetes (a disease of the mind), but by the effect of the insulin and not eating. It could be automatism (the insulin being an external factor) but it is debateable whether this would succeed. In **Quick** the court said 'self-induced' incapacity would not excuse and suggested this would include failing to take regular meals. However, in **Baillie,** the court suggested that although voluntarily consuming drink or drugs would not excuse, failing to take regular meals might. The comment was only* obiter *(because there was anyway insufficient loss of control) so the situation is not clear. If the automatism defence succeeds she will be acquitted.*

An owl flew into Dan's windscreen causing him to swerve and ...

*This suggests automatism because, like the hypothetical situation of the swarm of bees in **Hill v Baxter**, it is an external factor which caused Dan to lose control. However, the fact that he swerved indicates that he did have at least some control over his actions. If this is the case, the defence will fail as in **Broome v Perkins 1987**. If Dan can show that his reaction was a purely automatic one however, he could succeed with the defence and be acquitted.*

Ahmed had been suffering from delusions, but the drugs his doctor gave him caused an unusual reaction and ...

*The word 'delusions' suggests the defence of insanity, however the fact that he was on prescribed drugs may mean he can use automatism. This is based on **Hardie**, where the court made a distinction between drugs meant to calm you and drugs known to cause unpredictable behaviour. The word 'unusual' here suggest the effect was not known and the drugs were prescribed by a doctor, so there was no 'self-induced' incapacity and Ahmed will be acquitted.*

Max had not been the same since he was hit on the head and suffered concussion, he panicked and...

Concussion would be automatism as it is an external factor. As he 'panicked' he may have been out of control. If the lack of control was total Max will be acquitted. There is some argument for insanity if the concussion was some time ago (the phrase is a little ambiguous) and had then led to a disease of the mind of some sort, such as pressure on the brain.

Tom was a diabetic who had not taken his insulin and during a fit he ...

*This would be insanity as the defect of reason (the fit) was caused by the diabetes (a disease of the mind) as in **Hennessey**. This means Tom is guilty by reason of insanity and will be subject to one of four orders.*

Imran had been driving so long he was in a semi-catatonic state and said he remembered nothing about the crash

*This suggests automatism as a semi-catatonic state would be an external factor. Much will depend on whether there was a total loss of control. In **Broome v Perkins 1987** it was held that as D was able to exercise some control, the defence was not available. There is also an argument that the loss of control is self-induced, as Imran did not have to drive for so long, so the defence will fail and he will be guilty of manslaughter.*

Arnie had been hearing voices which told him all unbelievers must die so he ...

*This would point to insanity, as hearing voices is a delusion and thus a defect of reason, likely to be caused by a disease of the mind. Much would then depend on what he knew at the time of the killing. According to the law from **Windle**, if Arnie knew that what he was doing was legally wrong, even if he believed it was morally right, he cannot use the defence so will be guilty of manslaughter.*

Henri was sent off for foul play (GBH s 20)

*The charge is GBH so this would indicate that he has caused serious harm but not with intent (or it would be **s 18**). He can use the defence of consent. It was said in **A-G's Reference (No 6 of 1980) 1981** that there is implied consent in 'properly conducted games and sports'. The defence succeeded in **Billingshurst** even though the conduct was outside the rules of the game, and in **Barnes** the court held that only conduct that was sufficiently grave to be deemed criminal could invalidate the defence in sporting cases. It would seem that Henri will succeed even though it was foul play.*

Jack thought he was being attacked and lashed out (battery)

*This indicates that Jack was mistaken but has used self-defence against the supposed attacker. He may succeed in this defence as it was made clear in **Williams** that he can rely on mistake to justify reasonable force. This is confirmed in **s 76** of the **Criminal Justice and Immigration Act**. As the charge was battery if harm was caused at all it was only minor, this suggest that only reasonable force was used.*

Rula got an infection after Tom gave her nose piercings (ABH)

*Tom can argue the defence of consent. Implied consent applies to 'reasonable surgical interference' (**A-G's Reference (No 6 of 1980)**). However, it is not clear whether she consented to harm. If the harm was serious and intentional, the defence could fail (**Dica/Brown**) but using **Richardson** and / or **Wilson** it may succeed. Finally, we are not told how old Rula is, and consent by a child may not be* valid. In **Burrell and Harmer 1967**, a 12- and 13-year-old were not deemed to have consented to actual bodily harm caused by tattooing. This could be applied here if Rula is not an adult.

As he came out of the night club Ben saw a man approach and lashed out (ABH)

*As with Jack, there is a mistaken belief that leads to the use of force in self-defence. However here Ben came out of a night club so there is a possibility he was intoxicated. If that is the reason he made the mistake the defence will fail. This was stated in **O'Grady** and confirmed by **s 76**.*

After taking several different drugs given to him by a friend Stefan went home to his girlfriend. In his confused state he totally flipped when she ran to hug him and thought she was a bear. He grabbed a knife and stabbed her (wounding with intent s 18)

*The best defence for Stefan would be automatism, because it results in an acquittal. However, although his lack of control was caused by an external factor and may have been total, self-induced automatism (e.g., caused by drink or drugs) will not succeed (**Lipman**). Although non-prescribed drugs were accepted in **Hardie** (because they were not known to be unpredictable) this is unlikely to be the case here as he took 'several different drugs' the effect of this is likely to be unpredictable. Stefan might instead argue intoxication or even self-defence. The latter will fail as stated above; a mistake can be unreasonable (**Williams**) but not drunken (**O'Grady**). As regards intoxication, this is voluntary so the **Majewski** rules apply. As **s 18** is a specific intent crime even if he succeeds in showing the intoxication meant he did not have mens rea, he will still be guilty of **s 20** wounding as he acted recklessly (**Majewski**).*

Mira begged the doctor to give her an injection to end her life (murder)

*Although Mira is consenting to her own death, it has been made clear in several cases that you cannot consent to murder. Thus, in **Cox**, the doctor could not use the defence of consent to excuse his actions and in **Pretty** the court refused to rule that her husband would not be prosecuted if he helped her to die. If the doctor agrees to her request, he will be guilty of murder.*

Exercise 29 Evaluation practice

This depends on which defences you chose. All five are covered in the answer to the examination question below and in the next section (though note you only needed reforms for one of the chosen defences).

Self-test questions

> The insanity rules come from **M'Naghten**
>
> It is automatism when the cause is external
>
> 'Dutch courage' is when D drinks to get up the nerve to carry out the crime and it does not provide a defence
>
> If D successfully pleads intoxication to a specific intent crime such as murder the result is that the conviction is for any relevant basic intent crime, for murder it would be manslaughter
>
> Two of the activities where consent is implied as stated in AG's Reference would be any two of the following:
>
>> properly conducted games and sports

lawful chastisement or correction

reasonable surgical interference

dangerous exhibitions

The conviction was quashed in **Barnes (2004)** because the conduct was not sufficiently grave to be classed as criminal

Self-defence was rejected by the jury in **Martin** because the force used was excessive and unreasonable

It was decided in **Hatton**, and confirmed by **s 76**, that D cannot rely on a mistaken belief caused by voluntary intoxication

Exercise 30 Examination practice

Write a critical analysis of any two of the general defences (insanity, automatism, intoxication, consent, self-defence/prevention of crime). Include in your answer a consideration of any proposals for reform of one of your chosen defences. (25 marks)

I have included two answers covering insanity and automatism, followed by consent and self-defence. Intoxication is discussed within these but a few criticisms of this defence follow separately, with a note of some relevant cases, which you could develop.

You can't cover everything so select a few of the points which make most sense to you and develop the cases a little to make them clearly relevant to what you say. As regards reforms, you were only asked to include these for one of your chosen defences so you can leave out the others I have covered.

Answer 1 (insanity and automatism)

*Problems with insanity centre on the age of the rules, which date from **M'Naghten's case 1843**. This means the definitions are antiquated and have not kept up with medical knowledge. The Law Commission identified insanity as an area in need of reform in its 10th Programme of law reform in 2008. In 2012 they produced a scoping paper, and anticipate publishing a further paper in 2013 taking into account responses to this.*

*The Law Commission say that the term 'insane' is "outdated" as a description of those with mental illness and "simply wrong" as regards those who have learning disabilities, learning difficulties or epilepsy. **Hennessey**, **Sullivan** and **Quick** can be used to highlight such problems. Current medical interpretations of insanity are very different to the way it was seen in 1843. The Law Commission notes that the law lags behind psychiatric understanding and that medical professionals do not apply the correct legal test. The core of the new project is to "identify better and more up to date legal tests and rules".*

The phrase 'disease of the mind' is arguably unclear and the LC notes that "it is hardly surprising that the rules have proved difficult to apply" and also says "the phrase has no agreed psychiatric meaning. As interpreted by the courts, it has even come to include conditions that are not mental disorders, such as epilepsy and diabetes". There clearly needs to be a medical definition of what amounts to a 'disease of the mind' in the 21st Century that will make sense to lawyers, the medical profession and, just as importantly, juries.

The Law Commission also notes that the problem with the case law on these two defences is that it is incoherent and produces results that run counter to common-sense (sleepwalking and diabetes cases can illustrate this). This could lead to a discussion of the distinction between 'internal' and 'external' factors used by the courts in finding which defence applies in the particular circumstances. Apart from this distinction, however, there is no clear division between the treatment of insanity and the treatment of automatism. The difference between not taking insulin, and taking it but not eating properly, is small, but leads to a huge difference for D, who is either found guilty by reason of *insanity or acquitted. The LC says the relationship between insanity and automatism needs to be addressed and that the relationship is unsatisfactory because of the 'external factor' doctrine, which it believes needs re-evaluating. Problems with this overlap can be seen in many cases such as **Quick**, **Sullivan**, **Hennessey** and **Bailey**, in particular as to whether failing to eat after taking insulin can mean it is 'self-induced' so that neither defence will succeed. The LC also shows concern over the complexity of the relationship between insanity and diminished responsibility and although the latter only applies to murder cases there still needs to be a clearer dividing line between these defences.*

Another problem is the stigma attached to being found 'insane'. As the LC points out, the current law is based on judicial rulings made in the first half of the nineteenth century. As a result, the legal tests consist of concepts on which there is no agreed psychiatric meaning. According to the LC a finding of insanity attracts huge stigma and it is a finding which, under the current law, may be made in cases where the defendant was not mentally disordered (again use cases on diabetes, epilepsy and/or sleepwalking to support the need for reform). Someone who should and could use the defence may well not do so because of this.

*You could go on to discuss the implications of a finding of not guilty by reason of insanity (one of four orders, which could include indefinite hospital treatment) and the difference with automatism (acquittal). This is a huge difference in outcomes when the two defences seem to overlap to such an extent. On a more positive note the law has improved as regards the orders which a judge can give. Until 1991 the only option was committal to a secure hospital for an indefinite period. The **Criminal Procedure (Insanity and Unfitness to Plead) Act 1991** increased a judge's powers in all cases except murder.*

*There are also arguments that the law on insanity could breach Article 5 of the **European Convention on Human Rights** which states that a person of unsound mind can only be detained where proper objective medical expertise has been sought, and this is mentioned in the introduction to the LC's new project as one of the reasons for the need to reform the law.*

Apart from the Law Commission, other suggestions for reform which can be discussed are those proposed by official bodies such as the Butler Committee, which favoured replacing the rules with a new verdict of 'mental disorder'. This would arise where D was suffering from 'severe mental illness' or 'severe mental handicap'. The LC points out that there has been no review of the criteria and terminology of insanity and unfitness to plead since the Butler Committee reported in 1975. The Law Commission's Draft Code had adopted many of the Butler Committee's recommendations e.g., to allow the defence of automatism rather than insanity for sleepwalking and spasms, so it is likely that the new project will also do so.

Go on to consider the problems with automatism as a separate issue. Although much has been included above there are also distinct issues and as you are asked to discuss two defences you need just a little more on this, and/or refer back to the particular issues relating to automatism already discussed. One criticism of the defence of automatism relates to the extent of the loss of control illustrated by cases such as **Attorney-General's Reference (No2 of 1992) 1994** and **Broome v Perkins 1987**. It may be hard for a jury to decide whether there was 'some awareness' or 'some control' in driving cases like this. In **Hill v Baxter** it was suggested that being attacked by a swarm of bees would mean automatism would be successful, but what if D attempted to take some avoiding action but still drove into and killed someone? Would trying to take avoiding action mean that D retained some control? If so, the defence would fail. Refer back to the problem of the somewhat irrational distinctions between external and internal factors and the fact that the defence overlaps with not only insanity but also diminished responsibility and loss of control.

A quote to end with (or start with) is useful – as long as it is appropriate and relevant – as it is always a good idea to start and finish strongly. Something like the following paragraph could provide a conclusion.

> In **Quick 1973**, Lawton LJ said the defence of insanity was a "quagmire of law seldom entered nowadays save by those in desperate need of some kind of defence". Nearly forty years later the Law Commission state that the defence is underused and the label 'insane' is "outdated" and, in some cases, "simply wrong". The law is clearly in need of real and urgent reform and it is to be hoped that, unlike earlier recommendations for reform, the new project will result in a positive response from the government followed by legislation by Parliament.

Answer 2 (Consent and self-defence)

The grounds for allowing or denying consent are not clear. In **Brown**, it was based on the level of harm caused, and the defence denied, but serious injuries were inflicted in **Aitken** and **Jones** and the defence was allowed. Properly conducted sports seems a fair base for allowing consent, but again in some sports there is a clear risk of serious harm, as in boxing and wrestling. In **Barnes**, the court held that only conduct that was sufficiently grave to be deemed criminal could invalidate the defence in sporting cases, and in **Billingshurst** the defence succeeded even though the conduct was outside the rules of the game. If the harm is both serious and intentional then it is at least questionable whether consent should be allowed. Also, it is not always clear whether an action is inside or outside the rules of the game and so inconsistency can result. Sometimes deliberate harm has been held acceptable and sometimes something unintentional, but reckless, results in a conviction.

There is no clear explanation of the reason for the decisions seen in the various cases. In **Dica** the decision rested on whether serious harm was intended whereas in **Brown** the judgements indicate that the decision was partly on whether harm was intended (mens rea) and partly on whether the harm was serious (actus reus). In **Dica**, where the decision was based on whether serious harm was intended, the CA said that consent could be a defence to recklessly inflicted injuries even if they were serious, which would cover 'rough horseplay' cases where the harm inflicted was not intentionally done, but recklessly. Also, there was no more 'real' consent by the victims in **Richardson** than there was in **Dica**. If the ruling in **Dica** was applied in all cases the defence would be more consistent. It probably would have failed in **Aitken** and **Richardson**, but may have succeeded in **Jones** if the actions were deemed reckless rather than intentional.

There are also problems in reconciling the decisions in **Brown** and **Wilson**. The decision in the former seems partly based on morality. It is arguably a restriction on personal freedom to make such consensual activities criminal and perhaps **Wilson** is to be preferred. Some would say that violence is socially unacceptable so that the law should interfere even though it is restricting people's freedom, thus would agree with the decision in **Brown**. On the other hand, it is arguable that what is done in the privacy of your own home should be a matter only for those involved and not the law, thus **Brown** was wrong. The decision in **Wilson** would perhaps also be seen as wrong to the first group of people, as it was an act of violence. However, this was between a man and his wife so it is more acceptable socially. This is a matter of opinion, as although it can be argued that an adult should be able to consent to harm, as long as that consent is real and based on all the facts, some would argue that violence of any kind is wrong. Where social opinion is divided, it is especially important for the law to be clear.

The 'rough horseplay' cases can be said to take implied consent too far. **Aitken** seems to go far beyond what can be justified as rough horseplay; it was a case of serious and unprovoked violent bullying. **Jones** is perhaps more understandable, as it was, arguably, more of a high-spirited game than bullying, although it can be said that it still went too far. Although (as suggested in **Dica** *above) consent is more acceptable where harm was recklessly inflicted, it is arguable that it should not apply to intentional serious harm. **Aitken** seems to have far less 'real' consent present than **Brown**, so either of these decisions can be criticised. Comparing **Brown** to **Aitken** and **Jones** provides no clear indication of where the courts will draw the boundaries on consent and serious harm, leaving the defence in an unsatisfactory state.*

*Another area which has caused difficulty is euthanasia cases where the victim is consenting to their own death, as in **Pretty**. So far, the courts have not gone so far as to allow consent in these cases but the decisions are sometimes hard to follow legally. In 2012, the High Court refused an application by a severely disabled man challenging the laws governing the right to die, saying it was for Parliament to decide. Parliament is, however, reluctant to address the issue as public opinion is so divided. The man, Mr Lamb, is to take his case to the Court of Appeal in 2013.*

*As regards reforms, these have not been very forthcoming by the courts, other than the decision in **Dica** to reject the defence in cases of intentional sexual diseases, which was a much needed reform because the law had come from the outdated case of **Clarence**. There is understandably a reluctance to be seen to interfere too much in people's personal freedoms, and there could be conflict with parts of the **European Convention on Human Rights**. However, if judges do not wish to be too creative then Parliament should act. It is anyway more appropriate for an elected Parliament to decide such policy issues.*

*The Law Commission's 2000 report on consent, although confined to sexual offences, aimed at producing a definition that would also be consistent with other offences. This report recommends that consent should be defined as "a subsisting, free and genuine agreement to the act in question" which could be express or implied, and "evidenced by words or conduct, whether present or past". It seems that it would be better for juries to have a clearer definition such as this as the law is unlikely to produce justice unless it is unambiguous and applicable to everyone in the same way. It would be beneficial if this definition were to be extended to consent as a defence for all offences, in particular the non-fatal offences. An agreement to the risk of serious harm would mean the defence could be used in a case such as **Brown**, the 'act in question' being GBH. However, the defence would fail in **Richardson** as the consent was not a "free and genuine agreement to the act in question".*

*If the proposed reforms were taken up, there would be an improvement in how the defence of consent is applied. It is time that Parliament legislated to clarify the issue and provide a definition of consent along the lines that the LC proposes but to apply to all offences, or at least to all non-fatal ones. In the meantime, if the courts were to apply the **Dica** ruling to all cases, not just cases of sexually transmitted diseases, there would be greater consistency and clarity in the law.*

*As regards self-defence, the 'all or nothing' nature of the defence can be a problem. D is either guilty or acquitted on what is sometimes a minor difference, especially when reacting due to a mistaken perception of the situation. It is arguable that self-defence should be a partial defence rather than a full one, certainly when used in defence of murder. A jury may be reluctant to accept the defence if it means D walks free after killing someone. There are also problems with the distinction between what is aggression and what is self-defence, particularly in relation to the question of whether D should have retreated if the possibility arose. In **McInnes 1971**, the CA said that a person is not obliged to retreat from a threat in order to rely on the defence, but it will be evidence for the jury when considering whether force was necessary, and if so whether it was reasonable. This means it is not fully clear whether the defence will be available to a D who doesn't run away, given the chance. What amounts to 'proportionate force' is also unclear, and cases such as **Clegg** and **Martin** illustrate this point. The issue of whether force was justified and whether force was reasonable in the circumstances is not fully divided. The first question is subjective; did D believe the action was justified? The second is objective; would a reasonable person (or the jury) see the force as reasonable in the circumstances? If D believed the action was justified but that belief is unreasonable the defence should still succeed. However, if the jury think it too daft to be seen as* reasonable it is unlikely they will acquit, adding an objective element to the first question. Perhaps the jury would be right to reject a totally unreasonable belief, but that is not what **Williams** and **s 76** provide; both say the belief can be unreasonable as long as genuine.

The Criminal Justice and Immigration Act 2008 has not reformed the law but makes it more transparent, as it puts into statute form many of the matters on self-defence dealt with at common law by the courts. **S 76(7)** confirms **Palmer 1971**, that D "may not be able to weigh to a nicety the exact measure of any necessary action" and that if D only did what was 'honestly and instinctively' thought to be necessary this would be strong evidence that only reasonable action was taken. **S 76(5)** now makes clear the ruling in **O'Grady** that the mistake needn't be a reasonable one, but it can't be a drunken one. In **O'Grady** D believed his friend was trying to kill him but the defence failed because he was drunk at the time. This seemed to be a matter of policy rather than principle (it is not in the public interest to allow D to rely on a drunken misconception of events), and so best left to Parliament rather than the courts. That the **Criminal Justice and Immigration Act 2008** has addressed the point is to be welcome.

The Act was "intended to clarify the operation of the existing defences", in particular, as to whether the degree of force used was reasonable in the circumstances. This question is to be decided by reference "to the circumstances as D believed them to be" but **s 76** further states that the degree of force used by D was not 'reasonable in the circumstances' if it was disproportionate. As stated above, this area is still a little unclear as regards how far the first question is really subjective.

Overall, the Act does not change the law but, as can be seen above, it has perhaps helped to clarify some of the judicial decisions as regards the requirements for self-defence to succeed as a defence. As time passes and more cases go to the higher courts, the effects of **s 76** may become even clearer.

Problems with Intoxication

Many of the problems with intoxication are seen when it is relevant to other defences, and these are discussed above. A few others follow.

In diminished responsibility, an abnormality of mental functioning caused by intoxication will not support the defence (**Dowds 2012**). However, alcoholism (a medical condition) may do (**Tandy 1989**). In this case, the jury can consider the drink but must ask whether it amounts to an abnormality (**Wood**). Where there is evidence of intoxication as well as another cause of 'abnormality' the jury should ignore the intoxication. This rule, from **Dietschmann 2003**, gives the jury an extremely difficult task.

With the defence of insanity, if the defect of reason comes about through intoxication, the insanity defence fails (**Lipman**). If the defect comes from alcoholism, it could succeed as this can be classed as a 'disease'.

With automatism, as D must be acting involuntarily the defence cannot be relied upon if the automatism was self-induced, e.g., by drinking or taking drugs, as in **Lipman**. Prescribed drugs would be OK and in **Hardie** the court accepted the defence where the drugs were **not** prescribed to D but he had expected them to calm him down, so the effects were unpredictable. Although this distinction is a little vague, in general most of these decisions appear sensible because it is not in the public interest to allow D to rely on being drunk to excuse the committing of a criminal offence.

The Law Commission, in its report on intoxication in 2009 (LC No 314), notes that the terms 'basic' and 'specific' intent are confusing and misleading. This distinction was made in **Majewski** but was not fully defined, so the issue was left unclear. **Majewski** was reconsidered in **Heard** but not clarified and the distinction is still confusing for lawyers and non-lawyers alike. The LC point out in their report that there is still no single test for deciding if an offence is one of basic or specific intent, so clearly there is a need for the law to be made unambiguous on this point. One reason for not *allowing intoxication to be used too widely is that it would mean that D can use being drunk to 'get away with' a crime, and this would not be in the public interest.*

On the whole, it can be said that the rule that voluntary intoxication should not provide a defence for criminal activities is a sensible one. However, some of the judicial decisions and reasoning remain obscure and more needs to be done to clarify these.

The following answers would all be higher-level but would need any shorthand to be written in full sentences. The examiner's comments are shaded, as here.

January 2012 Scenario 2

04 plan

Identify the offence(s)

Harry: Lauren's injury is a permanent scarring so the appropriate offence is wounding or inflicting / causing grievous bodily harm under **s 20** or **s 18** of the **Offences against the Person Act 1861 (OAPA)**.

Define them and explain / apply the AR/MR

*Wounding requires that the skin is broken according to **C v Eisenhower**. Grievous bodily harm is defined in **Smith** as really serious harm, but in **Saunders** it was said that it was enough that the harm was serious. As her arms are 'ripped' and she has 'permanent scarring' this will satisfy the AR of wounding because permanent scars would not occur if both layers of the skin were not broken. Also the harm is serious enough to be grievous bodily harm. The chain of causation will not be broken by her flinging herself into a hedge as this is foreseeable – it is similar to **Roberts** where the girl jumped out of the car and this did not break the chain. It has been held that the words inflict and cause mean the same thing so Harry could be charged with either **s 20** or **s 18**. Even though the problem originated with James and Harry was not the sole cause of the harm, he drove at them for a joke and so made a significant contribution to the result (**Cheshire**).*

*MR for **s 20** is intent or subjective recklessness as to some harm, not serious harm – **Mowatt**. He did not seem to intend any harm at all but driving at someone is dangerous and he must have realised there was a risk of at least some harm and carried on so was reckless – **Cunningham**.*

*It will not be **s 18** as the MR for this is intent (only) to cause grievous bodily harm (**Parmenter**).*

There is a possible argument for **s 47** but this would not be enough alone as the injury is serious. As this question covers manslaughter as well as this injury, and time is limited, it is fine to discuss only **s 20** here. This is the most appropriate charge as regards the injury, so is enough on its own.

*Harry: Unlawful act manslaughter – AR is an unlawful and dangerous act causing death. The unlawful act is assault. This is to intentionally or recklessly cause the victim to apprehend immediate personal violence. However 'Kim realised that it was Harry and began to laugh' so if she was not in fear there may be no AR for an assault, as in **Lamb** where the friend was not afraid – therefore no unlawful act. Maybe when the wheel came off she was afraid, if so there is AR. The MR is that for the unlawful act, there is no need to intend or be reckless as to the death. He had MR as he intended to scare her, and MR and AR coincide as the MR can be continuing and connect to the earlier AR as was the case (but the other way round) in **Fagan**.*

Note that the question says the charge is involuntary manslaughter so no there is no need to consider murder; the only thing is to decide which type of involuntary manslaughter it is.

*If Harry did commit an unlawful act the next thing is whether it was dangerous. Would reasonable people see it as such – **Church**? Driving at someone, even as a joke, is likely to be seen as dangerous by most people so this is satisfied. The unlawful and dangerous act must cause death – as above – even if not the sole cause he made a significant contribution (**Cheshire**). If assault is proved unlawful act manslaughter is likely to succeed. If not there is a possible alternative in gross negligence manslaughter as he created a dangerous situation – **Miller** – and failed to do anything about it. He owed duty to road-users and breached it by driving in that way. There is a risk of death when* *driving at someone so the only question is whether the jury believe his action to be sufficiently bad to be deemed criminal, which is quite likely.*

There is a lot to cover in this question so the lack of detail on the alternative charge will not detract from high marks. The most likely offence, unlawful act manslaughter is dealt with well.

*James: Gross negligence manslaughter. This can be by an omission if there is a duty to act. **Adomako** test – duty + breach + gross negligence. Duty and breach are as for civil law. Here there is a contractual duty as in **Pittwood**. As for breach, he did not do what a reasonable person would have done. A reasonable mechanic would have tightened the nuts properly. Also **Misra** – there must be a risk of death not just harm. There is always a risk of death if a car is not properly maintained as it can kill other road users. As regards gross negligence, the conduct must be so bad in all the circumstances that the jury believe it to be criminal. This is not certain as it is a matter for the jury, but a mechanic not tightening the nuts would be like an anaesthetist not monitoring a patient as in **Adomako**. The failure to act caused death as 'but for' his failure she would not have died (**White**) and even if not the sole cause (Harry was also partly the cause) he significantly contributed to the death (**Cheshire**). Harry's driving may also have contributed but is unlikely to break the chain of causation because even if he had driven normally the wheel could have foreseeably come off. If the jury believe his omission was sufficiently bad to be deemed criminal James may be guilty.*

This answer accurately explains and applies the law and, although saying it is a matter for the jury, makes a good attempt at reaching a conclusion with a comparison to the anaesthetist in **Adomako**. There is good reference to the given facts throughout.

05 Plan

*Murder is the unlawful killing of a human being. AR seems straightforward but Did Mike's actions cause death? **White / Cheshire***

*Factually he did as 'but for' his actions Oliver would not have died. Legally he made a significant contribution as did the attacker in **Cheshire**. Oliver's weak skull brings in the 'thin-skull rule'. This says D must 'take his victim as he finds him' – **Blaue**, so this weakness does not break the chain of causation. The second issue on causation is the switching off of the life-support machine. In **Malcherek & Steele** this did not break the chain, nor did withdrawing food and treatment in **Bland**, so Mike is still liable for the death. Hospital treatment very rarely breaks the chain – **Cheshire***

*MR is intent to kill or seriously injure – **DPP v Smith 1961**. Direct intent is where death or serious injury is his aim or purpose (**Mohan**). Mike stamped 'three or four times' on Oliver's head so there is direct intent at least to cause serious injury. Even if not, indirect intent can be established. The test from **Nedrick/Woollin** is that indirect intent can be found if death or serious injury is virtually certain and D appreciates this.*

*It seems Mike has both AR & MR of murder. Possible defence under **the Homicide Act 1957** or the **Coroners and Justice Act 2009**. Either would reduce his conviction to manslaughter.*

This is a good plan covering both the issues of causation, with several references to the facts and appropriate cases in support. The issue of intent does not need any more detail, the main points are dealt with well and it is anyway reasonably clear.

Apply the rules on diminished responsibility and / or loss of control as appropriate

*Diminished responsibility – **s 2** of the **1957 Act** as amended by **s 52** of the **2009 Act**. There must be an abnormality of mental functioning. This must have substantially impaired his ability to understand what he was doing, form a rational judgment or to exercise self-control and must arise from a recognised medical condition. He will need expert medical evidence to show his anxiety and stress were sufficient. Abnormality was said in **Byrne** to be something any reasonable person would* *see as abnormal and this may be the case here. Impairment must be more than trivial but not necessarily total – **Lloyd**. He seems to know what he is doing but his stress may have impaired his ability to form a rational judgement or to exercise control, although not fully clear. Finally, it must provide a reason for his conduct – a matter of causation and this seems to be the case. As he was in a bar it may be that the abnormality was partly caused by drink. If so, the jury must ignore this – **Dietschmann**.*

Again, this is a good plan with accurate law and relevant cases. The application is sufficiently well done, improved by the fact that it was noticed that there could be an intoxication issue.

*Loss of control – **s 54** of the **2009 Act**. Mike must have lost self-control due to a qualifying trigger. A person of his age and sex, with a normal degree of tolerance and self-restraint, might have reacted in a similar way. He may have lost control because of 'things said' by Oliver. Although this is a qualifying trigger it must also amount to circumstances of an 'extremely grave character' and have caused Mike to have a 'justifiable sense of being seriously wronged'. The comments about having sex with Nora and about his daughter could both be sufficiently serious and make him feel justifiably wronged. Sexual infidelity is excluded as a trigger by **s 55** of the **Act**, but it was said in **Clinton 2012** that it could be taken into account as part of the overall circumstances. He can therefore rely on the second comment as the trigger for his loss of control but with the first comment providing further evidence to strengthen his defence as to why he lost control.*

Before the Act, his defence may have failed on the requirement for any loss of control to be 'sudden and temporary' but this is no longer the law, so the 45-minute delay will not mean he cannot use this defence. A person of his age and sex may have acted the same way in his particular circumstances (though we cannot include his irritability as a characteristic of the reasonable person); if the jury believe this to be the case, his defence will succeed.

This answer shows the new law has been well understood. It is clearly stated with sufficient detail and is well applied to the facts, with reference to one of the few cases heard since the **2009 Act**.

06 Plan

*The mens rea for murder is intent to kill or seriously injure, for such a serious crime it should be intent to kill. The law on intent has been developed by judges but is arguably still unclear despite the **Nedrick** direction. Murder is a common law offence; there should be a statutory definition with more than one degree of murder as the LC recommended. This could allow for a discretionary sentence in all but the killing of someone with intent.*

Diminished responsibility is not a satisfactory alternative for abused women as it indicates they are mentally unbalanced. A 'recognised medical condition' perhaps is better as it would not be limited to mental issues, but there still has to be an impairment of mental functioning.

*Where there is evidence of intoxication as well as another cause of 'abnormality' the jury has to perform an almost impossible task of separating the one from the other – **Dietschmann** – the new law does not change this.*

'Abnormality of mental functioning' is difficult for the jury to understand and medical evidence is often complex and contradictory. It is not clear whether the new law has helped other than requiring a recognised medical condition.

*The difficulties of these defences for the jury could lead to inconsistency. Juries may differ in their decisions. Whether diminished responsibility succeeds as a defence is sometimes dependent on whether the killing was morally wrong – **Bailey/Sutcliffe**.*

*Success may depend on which defence is raised in the first place. What was then provocation failed in the case of **Cocker 1989**, but diminished responsibility succeeded in **Bailey 2002** in similar circumstances.*

*There is an overlap between diminished responsibility and loss of control where the killing has been due to a mental state such as depression or long-term abuse (**Aluwahlia** and **Thornton**).*

Loss of control is still required, against the LC's recommendations, so abused women cases may still fail even though it was cases like these that prompted calls for changes to the old law.

The removal of the need for a 'sudden and temporary' loss of control is an improvement. However, the fact that any loss of control must be shown goes against the Law Commission's proposals and prevents the defence clearly extending to cases of abuse against women. Also the fact that acting in a desire for revenge is excluded arguably brings back an element of the 'sudden and temporary' requirement.

The inclusion of a fear of serious violence as a qualifying trigger may solve some of the problems with the 'all or nothing' nature of self-defence where juries may be reluctant to accept it, feeling that D should not be totally acquitted. In a murder case, the loss of control defence may be a more suitable alternative as D is not acquitted but sentenced at the judge's discretion.

*Overall, although there have been some improvements and reference to a recognised medical condition is clearer than the old law, there are still problems. Developmental immaturity in those under 18 should be included as the Law Commission recommended. Also for loss of control there should not be so many restrictions such as excluding sexual infidelity and requiring things done or said to be extremely grave and lead to a justifiable sense of being seriously wronged. Finally, the need for loss of control, which was not recommended by the Law Commission, may mean that many cases where the law was intended to help will still fail, such as abused women like **Thornton**.*

This answer has picked up on many of the problems with murder and the partial defences and has made a solid attempt at identifying where problems remain, as well as noting where improvements have been made. The concluding paragraph is strong, clearly referring to the question asked by pulling together some of the improvements and remaining problems previously discussed.

January 2010 Scenario 1

The middle-level answer lacks detail of the offences, little statutory authority and is somewhat weak in application. There is little reference to the facts for battery / ABH e.g., although it says he caused more than trivial harm there is no mention of the 'red marks' or 'swelling'. The irrelevant discussion of sentencing and causation would not lose marks specifically, but this has used up time that should have been spent on a better explanation and application. The *mens rea* is weak as it suggests MR for ABH is needed for some kind of harm rather than just for the battery, and the type of harm is not mentioned for the MR for **s 18** and **20** (although there is at least a reference to the facts on the *mens rea* issue). **S 18** is a little better but transferred malice is not mentioned. Consent is dealt with too briefly in both cases, but again there is better reference to the facts.

What follows would be an A* answer.

Plan

Henry: battery and ABH under s 47. MR for battery only – Savage. Defence of consent – possible rough horseplay – Jones

Jack: Wounding under s 18 or s 20. Issue of intent for s 18. Transferred malice. Consent – serious harm – Brown. Unlikely to be 'properly organised' sport – A-Gs Reference

*01 The 'red marks' and 'small swelling' Henry inflicted on Jack were at least a battery. However, although fairly minor, the harm is likely to have amounted to a 'more than merely trivial hurt or injury' (Chan Fook). This means an assault occasioning actual bodily harm under the **Offences against the Person Act 1861 s 47** is a more appropriate offence. The actus reus is an assault or battery which results in some harm occurring. The mens rea required for s 47 is the same as the* mens rea *for battery, there is no need to show mens rea as regards any harm. This was confirmed in* **Savage**.

Hitting someone in the face is a battery and, even though he wore a blindfold, he intended to apply unlawful force, as it was a boxing match. At the very least he must have recognised the risk of touching Jack (and even touching clothes is enough for a battery as decided in **Thomas**) *and so was reckless. Henry therefore has the* mens rea *for a battery, and the fact that the battery resulted in harm provides the necessary* actus reus *for* **s 47**, *an assault (which includes a battery) occasioning actual bodily harm, to be proved. No further mens rea is needed and there is no causation issue.*

The injury to Karim was a wound, this was described in **Eisenhower** *as a break in both layers of the skin and as it is a 'deep cut' this will be the case here. Whether Jack is charged under* **s 18** *or* **s 20** *of the Act will depend on* mens rea, *the* actus reus *is essentially the same. For* **s 20** *wounding or inflicting grievous bodily harm, it is only required that Jack intends or is reckless as to 'some' harm* (**Mowatt**). *This would not be hard to prove as he used a knife. He may not have intended or been reckless as regards causing any harm to Karim, but he lashed out at Jack so the* mens rea *for this can be transferred to Karim under the doctrine of transferred malice as decided in* **Latimer**. *This means the intent to inflict 'some harm' on Jack can be transferred to Karim, providing both the* actus reus *and* mens rea *of* **s 20**. *The use of the knife could bring it within* **s 18** *as it could indicate that he intended to cause Jack serious harm, which is needed for* **s 18** *as decided in* **Parmenter**. *He may be charged with wounding with intent under* **s 18**. *Again, transferred malice can be used to make him liable for Karim's injuries. If intent cannot be proved the jury can bring in a verdict under* **s 20**, *this was confirmed in* **Savage**.

Henry may be able to plead the defence of consent. It would have to be shown that Jack consented to the risk of harm, and did so freely. This would be a defence to a battery but it is more arguable whether it will succeed as regards any actual bodily harm (**Brown**). *In* **AG's Reference (No 6 of 1980) 1981** *the court set out several matters which could indicate implied consent and these included 'properly conducted games and sports'. The boxing match between Henry and Jack is not likely to be viewed as 'properly conducted' though, especially as they did not wear two boxing gloves, only one. This means it is more likely to be seen as a fist fight so that the defence would fail for the same reasons as those set out in* **AG's Reference**. *However, it is possible the fight could be seen as 'rough horseplay'. The defence has succeeded even when injuries were serious. In both* **Jones** & **Aitken** *the injuries were serious but the defence was still accepted, so this could be the case here, even though in* **Brown** *it was suggested that you could not consent to serious harm. If it is accepted as rough horseplay then Jack will be deemed to have consented to the risk of injury and Henry will be found not guilty of the battery or ABH charge.*

As regards Jack's offence, the defence is unlikely to succeed. The injury to Karim was a wound, and **Brown** *suggests that consent cannot be argued where the harm is serious. Also, in* **Dica**, *although a case involving sexually transmitted disease, it was held that if serious harm was intended the defence would fail. If this was applied to intentional serious harm in general then if Jack is charged under* **s 18** *the defence will fail. If charged under* **s 20** *the situation is less clear, but if Brown is followed, it could fail here too. It is anyway debateable whether watching the boxing match could amount to consenting to the risk of harm; she was not a participant in the game like Jack. The use of a knife would also take the situation outside any possible consent to accept the risk of harm; Karim certainly did not consent to that type of harm. I believe that the defence would fail and Jack would be guilty of wounding.*

This is a really good higher-level response. The appropriate offences are discussed in sufficient detail, with good reference to the given facts and relevant cases in support. *Mens rea* is dealt with accurately in each case and applied to the given facts. The defence of consent is dealt with correctly (students often fail to go on to consider defences, which will lower their possible marks), and again the rules are well explained with relevant case authority, and clearly applied to the facts by directly quoting from the scenario.

02

The middle-level answer on murder partially defines the *actus reus* and *mens rea* of murder but the explanation of *mens rea* is incomplete. There is also insufficient application and little reference to the given facts. Although when it is an issue for the jury it is permissible not to be absolute in the conclusion there needs to be an attempt to apply the law before saying it could go either way.

The law on loss of control is generally accurate apart from the incorrect Act (it should be the **Coroners and Justice Act 2009**) but not fully explained, especially as regards the restrictions on the qualifying triggers. There is an attempt at application to the facts but it is not enough to raise the level because there is insufficient explanation on which to base this.

The answer on diminished responsibility makes an attempt at application with some reference to the facts but the defence is not sufficiently explained. Substantial impaired is mentioned but not developed and it is not applied to the facts. There is no conclusion as to whether the defence might succeed.

Plan

Murder, AR / MR. Intent to seriously harm enough – Smith. Nedrick test for indirect intent.

Loss of control. Partial defence to murder – s 54 & s55 CJA 2009 – reduces to manslaughter. Qualifying trigger – fear of violence or things done/said – but must be extremely grave / give justifiable sense of being seriously wronged. Loss of control need not be sudden – S 54(2)

Diminished responsibility – also partial defence. S2 Homicide Act 1957 as amended. Abnormality of mental functioning – Byrne. Recognised medical condition. Substantial impairment – Lloyd –of ability to understand the nature of his conduct, form a rational judgment or exercise self-control

> *Murder is the unlawful killing of a human being. Mike pushed Pete over the railing which is unlawful and caused Pete's death, so this appears to fulfil the* actus reus. *On the given facts, causation is not an issue. The main issue is* mens rea. *The* mens rea *of murder is intent to kill or seriously injure (**Smith**). As death or serious injury is probably not Mike's aim or purpose, as described in **Mohan**, it may be hard to prove direct intent, but indirect intent is possible. The law on indirect intent comes from **Nedrick** and was confirmed by the House of Lords in **Woollin**. Death or serious injury as a result of D's actions must be a virtual certainty, and D must appreciate this. It is a virtual certainty that if a person is pushed and falls from the upper level of a shopping centre, they will be at least be seriously injured if not die. If the jury 'find' that Mike appreciated this then he has the necessary* mens rea *for murder, as in **Matthews & Alleyne** where the D's pushed someone in a river knowing he could not swim. It is arguable either way because Mike was delusional so even though the first part of the test is satisfied the second part is more doubtful. The jury may well believe that Mike did not appreciate that death or serious injury was a virtual certainty. However, if* mens rea *is established he may be able to use a partial defence to the murder charge. Firstly, Mike could claim loss of control under **s 54 & s 55** of the **Coroners and Justice Act 2009**. There are three questions to consider for this defence.*

> *Did Mike lose self-control (and did the killing result from this)?*

> *Did the loss of self-control have a qualifying trigger (as specified in **s 55**)?*

> *Would a person of Mike's sex and age with a normal degree of self-restraint have reacted in the same way as D in those circumstances?*

> *It would seem that Mike lost control as he 'suddenly ran at him'. **S 55** states that the loss of control must have a qualifying trigger; one such trigger is a fear of violence. Mike felt his life was in danger*

but whether he felt this at the time he lost control is unclear. The other qualifying trigger in *s 55* is 'things done or said', and Pete has shouted at him and called him a 'stupid old idiot' so this would be 'things said'. **S 55** further states that these must have constituted circumstances of an extremely grave character, and have caused Mike to have a justifiable sense of being seriously wronged. It is unclear whether Pete's words are sufficient to satisfy these points. If they do then the last question is whether another person of the same age and sex would have reacted the same way in the circumstances. The **Coroners and Justice Act** puts the reasoning in **Holley** into statutory form so that mental characteristics are not taken into account in this question. However, his medical history may be relevant as a 'circumstance'; this was the case in **Clinton** as regards sexual infidelity – even though excluded by the Act as a trigger it was said to be 'part of the whole'. Anything like a short-temper which affects his ability to show self-restraint, will be irrelevant. Apart from reference to a 'number of arguments' there is no real evidence of this, so the jury may decide that another person would have done the same if in his circumstances, with his medical history being part of those circumstances. The Act states that the loss of self-control does not need to be sudden as was the case before the reforms – *s 54(2)*. The fact that he ran at Pete 'a few minutes later' will not mean the defence fails. However, that and the fact that Pete was walking away may convince a jury that Mike had not lost control at all.

He could plead diminished responsibility, which would also reduce his conviction from murder to manslaughter. This is found in *s 2 Homicide Act 1957* as amended by the **Coroners and Justice Act 2009**. There are three points to consider. Firstly, there must be an abnormality of mental functioning. This was said in **Byrne** to be something that a reasonable man would see as abnormal and although the definition has changed from abnormality of mind to abnormality of mental functioning it is likely that the **Byrne** interpretation still applies. His belief that he is being followed was 'wholly unjustified' so would be likely to be deemed abnormal. Secondly, this abnormality must arise from a recognised medical condition. He should be able to obtain medical evidence that he has some form of paranoia and that this is such a condition. Thirdly, the abnormality must substantially impair his ability to understand the nature of his conduct, form a rational judgment or exercise self-control.

The cases under the old law will help decide what is 'substantial', in **Lloyd** the court held that it did not mean total but must be more than trivial. It would appear that Mike's abnormality has sufficiently impaired his ability to form a rational judgment to be seen as substantial. There is a final issue on top of these three points, which is that the abnormality 'provides an explanation' for Mike's actions, which means it caused him to act as he did. It is not clear whether his belief that Pete was following him caused him to kill as he attacked him as he was walking off. If his abnormality of mental functioning, even though substantial, did not cause him to kill Pete then the defence will fail and he will be guilty of murder. However, the defence may succeed as the events were all fairly closely connected, in which case he will be convicted of manslaughter.

Again this is a really good higher-level answer. The law is clearly set out with relevant case authority and the application is excellent, with plenty of direct references to the given facts. The lack of a definitive conclusion does not detract from the answer as the *mens rea* for murder is a matter for the jury, who may or may not 'find' intent. Also, once the judge has ruled there is evidence to support either of the two partial defences, it is then up to the jury, and whether either will be accepted is not certain.

N.B.: There is an arguable case for the insanity defence as an alternative to diminished responsibility and this would receive equal credit

03

The middle-level answer makes some good points about the problems but these are not usually well-developed. The answer ignores the requirement to discuss the proposed reforms and this type of omission will seriously affect the marks. Although the reforms to voluntary manslaughter have taken place since the question was set, not only the proposals but the Act were already in place.

Plan

Explanation of the criticisms of the current law on murder

Explanation of the criticisms of the current law on the partial defences of loss of control and / or diminished responsibility

Discussion of reforms of murder and / or the defences

You would not have time to cover all the following points but here is a fairly comprehensive list of criticisms, along with some improvements and possible reforms. I have included more than you need so you can choose those that you feel you can best explain. You only need to aim for about half the content. You do not even need to address all three, but must include discussion of murder and at least one of the partial defences. Most importantly to get into the higher grades you need to include some discussion of reforms.

Note that this answer was written after the reforms took place.

Murder

*The current law on murder is not set out in an Act of Parliament but comes from case law. Sometimes the law is not clear. The law on intent has developed but along the way, there were many different definitions using words like foreseeable, natural consequence, probable, highly probable etc. In **Woollin** Lord Hope said there was a need for a direction which is both 'clear and simple' and added that "the **Nedrick** direction fulfils this requirement admirably". This refers to the current law that intent can be found if, at the time of acting, D appreciated that death or serious injury was a virtually certain result of that action. This was later confirmed by the HL in **Woollin**. Lord Hope seems to think the law is more satisfactory since this test and possibly he is right, as it has been used in **Matthews & Alleyne** to find intent where the Ds knew the victim could not swim. However it has not always been used consistently and the law would be better if set out clearly in an Act of Parliament.*

*Also on mens rea, it is arguable that for such a serious crime as murder it should only be intent to kill and not to kill or seriously injure. It does not seem right that someone can be convicted of murder where the intent is to cause serious harm rather than death, as the current law states – **DPP v Smith**. The Law Lords criticised the rule in **Cunningham 1981** but refused to overrule it, preferring to leave that to Parliament. It is time that a government attempted to clarify the law and put a bill before Parliament as suggested by the Law Commission.*

*Sometimes questions arise about whether someone who is 'brain dead' or a foetus in the womb is a human being. In **AGs Reference (No 3 of 1994) 1997**, the HL held that a foetus was not a human being for the purpose of a murder conviction. However, if the foetus is injured and dies from that injury after being born, that could amount to murder. Arguably, there should be greater clarity on this.*

*Another problem with the current law on murder is with euthanasia, or 'mercy killing'. Under the current law, killing a loved one who is suffering and begs for relief from the pain will be murder, as the aim or purpose is to kill, so there will be direct intent. Perhaps the law should differentiate between different types of killing but it is controversial and people have strong opinions on both sides which makes a government reluctant to act. Also, the law sometimes seems to be based on morality rather than following legal rules. In **Airedale NHS Trust v Bland**, it was not murder for doctors intentionally to withhold food, but in **Gibbins & Proctor** it was murder when parents did so.*

***Bland** can be compared to **Cox 1992**, where a doctor gave an injection to a patient begging for help to die. The HL in **Bland** made clear that the ruling would not extend to a positive act. Juries may* make their decision on moral grounds, because they are sympathetic to the difficulties faced by a person being asked to help end a painful existence, so they may acquit when D clearly had an intention to kill. This means the judge cannot pass sentence at all. The cases of **Inglis** and **Gilderdale** highlight this problem because one woman was convicted of murder and the other had a suspended sentence on the similar facts of killing a child.

If the mandatory sentence for murder was abolished some of these problems would be resolved because the judge could take the circumstances into account.

Diminished responsibility

It is wrong that the accused must prove the defence as generally the burden of proof is on the prosecution.

This is not a satisfactory alternative to loss of control for abused women as it indicates they are mentally unbalanced.

Where there is evidence of intoxication as well as another cause of 'abnormality' the jury has to perform an almost impossible task of separating the one from the other – **Dietschmann**.

Diminished responsibility is sometimes dependent on whether the killing was morally wrong – **Bailey/Sutcliffe.**

The abnormality must have substantially impaired D's ability to understand the nature of his conduct, form a rational judgement or exercise self-control. This is the narrower than the old law and may exclude people to whom it was intended to apply (e.g., **Thornton**).

One improvement is the reference to a recognised medical condition. This is clearer than the old law on diminished responsibility, but 'abnormality of mental functioning' is still difficult for the jury to understand and medical evidence is often complex and contradictory. Another problem is that the Law Commission recommended that developmental immaturity in those under 18 should be included as a recognised medical condition. This was because there is evidence to show that parts of the brain which play an important role in the development of self-control do not mature until 14 years of age. However, the Government did not act on this suggestion.

Loss of control

The removal of the need for a 'sudden and temporary' loss of control is an improvement. However, the fact that any loss of control must be shown goes against the Law Commission's proposals and may prevent the defence extending to cases of abuse against women, who may be physically weaker and liable to even greater abuse if they lose control and fight back. It was cases like this that prompted calls for changes to the old law but in many cases nothing will have changed.

One problem with both the need for loss of control and the exclusion of acting in a desire for revenge, is that these arguably bring back an element of the 'sudden and temporary' requirement because a lapse of time will indicate that D has either not lost control or has had time to plan revenge.

The inclusion of a fear of serious violence as a qualifying trigger may help in cases where someone is reacting to violence but doesn't meet the requirements for the defence of self-defence. It could solve some of the problems with the 'all or nothing' nature of self-defence where juries may be reluctant to accept it feeling that D should not be totally acquitted. In a murder case the loss of control defence may be a more suitable alternative as D is not acquitted but sentenced at the judge's discretion. This is therefore an improvement but the law is stricter than the LC envisaged. The triggers are quite strict as if D relies on things done or said these have to be 'extremely grave' and give a 'justifiable sense of being seriously wronged'. Previously D could rely on things done or said without these restrictions so I feel this is a negative reform.

It is also unclear why sexual infidelity was excluded as a trigger as this type of situation was what led to the original defence of provocation. It is also a difficult concept to define which could lead to inconsistent jury decisions. On a positive note, judges may assist in addressing remaining defects when interpreting the new law, as in **Clinton**, where the CA held that sexual infidelity could be taken into account as part of the overall circumstances when deciding if someone else would have reacted in a similar way.

Possible conclusion

I feel that there should be a statutory definition of murder, perhaps a three-tiered structure, as the LC recommend. Only murder with intent to kill would mean a life-sentence, if only serious harm was intended sentencing would be discretionary, as also with the partial defences. I think the law has improved with regard to diminished responsibility but it is stricter than the LC had recommended and should have allowed for developmental immaturity. Also, despite some improvement, the defence of loss of control is too strict. Particularly as regards the triggers, but also as regards the need for a loss of control because a person that loses control in certain circumstances, e.g., an abused wife, is not such a danger to the public as a cold-blooded killer. As for sexual infidelity, if this were not excluded judges would not have to interpret the law to try and do justice in the circumstances as happened in **Clinton**. For such a serious offence the law needs to be clear and consistent and made by an elected Parliament.

www.ingramcontent.com/pod-product-compliance
Lightning Source LLC
Chambersburg PA
CBHW060148200526
45165CB00023B/1332